WHY WE MAKE THINGS AND WHY IT MATTERS

WHY WE MAKE THINGS AND WHY IT MATTERS
The Education of a Craftsman

PETER KORN

■ SQUARE PEG

Published by Square Peg 2015

2 4 6 8 10 9 7 5 3 1

Copyright © Peter Korn 2013

First published in the United States by David R. Godine, New Hampshire

First published in Great Britain in 2015 by
Square Peg
Vintage Books, 20 Vauxhall Bridge Road,
London SW1V 2SA

www.vintage-books.co.uk

A Penguin Random House Company

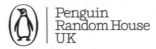

www. Penguinrandomhouse.com

A CIP catalogue record for this book
is available from the British Library

ISBN 9780224101097

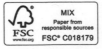 Penguin Random House is committed to a
sustainable future for our business, our readers
and our planet. This book is made from Forest
Stewardship Council® certified paper.

Printed and bound in Great Britain by Clays Ltd, St Ives PLC

Contents

WHO KNOWS what form the forward momentum of life will take in the time ahead or what use it will make of our anguished searching. The most that any one of us can seem to do is to fashion something— an object or ourselves—and drop it into the confusion, make an offering of it, so to speak, to the life force.

ERNEST BECKER, *The Denial of Death*

Introduction

I BELONG TO a generation of furniture makers to whom woodworking initially presented itself as a lost art from a more authentic time. When I turned my first clear pine board into a cradle, and for many years thereafter, I was beguiled by rediscovering the *how* of craft. How do you sharpen a chisel? How do you cut a sliding dovetail? How do you make a chair comfortable? Eventually, though, I also began to wonder about the *why*. What is craft and why does it matter? Why do we make things? Or, more specifically, why do we choose the spiritually, emotionally, and physically demanding work of bringing new objects into the world with creativity and skill?

The answers I have found – through considering the work of my own hands, through the practical education of a life in craft, and through the shared experiences of others – all seem to lead back to one fundamental truth: we practice contemporary craft as a process of self-transformation. Why this should be so and what its ramifications are, not only for craft and other creative fields, but also for understanding our own humanity, is the subject of this book.

More than five years ago I told myself that if I put down at least one word a day about the things that deeply mattered to me, I would be ahead of where I was not writing about them at all. My previous efforts as an author had been in the how-to genre. Books such as *The Woodworker's Guide to Handtools* (Taunton Press, 1998) and *Woodworking Basics: Mastering the Essentials of Craftsmanship* (Taunton Press, 2003) were relatively straightforward to write. I knew in advance the material I had to cover, so all I needed to do was construct a thorough outline and put flesh on the bones as clearly and accurately as possible. Not so this book! The slow, focused work of translating elusive perceptions about the *why* of craft into language, one tentative word at a time, has taken surprising turns. Every statement has provoked new questions, until finally I have found myself mapping out terrain hitherto invisible to me. I could never have imagined, for example, the extent to which I now see individuality as an illusion, the formation of identity as a full-time project, and thought as a phenomenon independent of language.

In short, writing this book has been a remarkable process of discovery. This is only fitting, since what I have come to see, bottom line, is that creative effort is a process of challenging embedded narratives of belief in order to think the world into being for oneself, and that the work involved in doing so provides a wellspring of spiritual fulfillment.

CHAPTER I

A Shared Hunger

THERE WAS A TIME when I assumed that becoming a master crafts-man would be a process of enlightenment. My hands were still igno-rant then, and I was searching for an occupation in which I could forge an adult self. Eager for competence, I thought that having one's craft together would mean having one's life together. Today, having become reasonably competent as a furniture maker, I know better. Spiritual enlightenment is not on the table. Still, the notions that drew me into the workshop forty years ago were not without con-sequence. The footing on which I started my journey has shaped my choices, concerns, and experiences throughout, and my transcendent expectations for a life in craft were rewarded in more palpable ways.

These days I teach more than I build. My students are adults from a wide variety of backgrounds, many with lives that could be consid-ered highly successful by any normative standard. Yet, consistently, I find that they have been drawn to woodworking by a hunger similar to that which first impelled me. They do not invest time, money, and effort traveling to Maine to cut dovetails with hand tools because they need little hardwood benches, which are the introductory-class projects. What lures them is the hope of finding a deeper meaning by learning to make things well with their own hands. Many go on to set up workshops of their own, and more than a few develop a pas-sion for woodworking they describe as transformational.

Beyond the red clapboard walls of our school I encounter many more people who express the same sort of longing. The banquet of work, leisure, and consumption that society prescribes has left some essential part of them undernourished. They are hungry for avenues of engagement that provide more wholesome sustenance.

The craft of furniture making is not a cure-all for this condition, but it functions as a source of meaning, authenticity, fulfillment – call it what you will, for the moment – for many people of my acquaintance. The same is true of other self-expressive, creative disciplines. They may not lead to the profound transfiguration to which I once vaguely aspired, yet their satisfactions are well matched to the earthly nature of our spiritual appetites. Furniture making, like all contemporary crafts, is a road less traveled. Yet it has much to reveal about the risks and rewards of sustained creative effort – about what art is and why it matters – in the context of our shared search for a better way to live.

Here I should mention three well-regarded authors who have already offered extracts of craft as antidotes to the spiritual deficiencies of modern life. Most iconic for my generation is Robert Pirsig, whose 1970s best seller, *Zen and the Art of Motorcycle Maintenance*, was presented as a meditation on the subject of quality. Pirsig lays out his central theme in describing how two young mechanics had carelessly repaired his bike:

> The mechanics in their attitude toward the machine were really taking no different attitude from the manual's toward the machine, or from the attitude I had when I brought it in there. We were all spectators. And it occurred to me there *is* no manual that deals with the *real* business of motorcycle maintenance, the most important aspect of all. Caring about what you are doing is considered either unimportant or taken for granted. On this trip I think we should notice it, explore it a little, to see if in that strange separation of what man is from what man does we may find some clues as to what the hell has gone wrong in this twentieth century.[1]

Pirsig's view, as he develops it, is that a good life may be found through craftsmanlike engagement with the actions, objects, and relationships of ordinary experience, through caring about what you do. If you choose to ride a motorcycle, then being able to repair a fouled spark plug becomes a moral imperative.

Thirty-five years later, sociologist Richard Sennett surveyed the same landscape from another station point in *The Craftsman*, where he asks what the process of making things reveals to us about ourselves. In particular, Sennett critiques current social and economic conditions for depriving workers of the satisfactions inherent to "doing a job well for its own sake," which is the essence he distills from craft. His solution is to cultivate an "aspiration for quality" in our workplaces and schools.[2] Like Pirsig, Sennett employs the ideal of quality, in the sense of caring about what one does, to address broad philosophical questions: What is the nature of work? What is the nature of a good life?

These same questions animate *Shop Class as Soulcraft,* in which author Matthew Crawford argues that our educational system and our occupational structures are deformed by a prejudice against manual labor. He punctures the myth of white-collar superiority by pointing out that today's corporate workplace has been rationalized as relentlessly as the industrial factory of a century earlier. Creative thought and decision making are centralized into the hands of small cohorts of experts, so that only rote work gets distributed among the worker bees. As a result, the average white-collar employee feels, accurately, like a replaceable cog in a soulless machine; work has been stripped of its potential to provide meaning and fulfillment. In counterpoint, Crawford asserts that significantly greater job satisfaction may be found in manual trades that engage a worker's cognitive, problem-solving abilities, such as his own vocation of motorcycle repair.

Although each identifies a different culprit, all three authors believe that some primary defect in contemporary culture severs the satisfactions of individual agency from the things that we actually do. (Broadly speaking, Pirsig faults the Aristotelian underpinnings of Western thought, Sennett faults the culture of corporate capitalism, and Crawford faults the pernicious effects of the Cartesian mind/body divide on education and the workplace.) Their indictments sound like nostalgia for a time when people found greater fulfillment in work because an aspiration to quality was ingrained. But, as any furniture maker who has looked at antiques with a skilled eye knows, quality has always been tailored to the cost constraints of time and materials. Really, what Pirsig, Sennett, and Crawford are asking is not where quality has gone, but how we can cultivate the aspiration for quality in today's world.

Several decades ago, as we were walking down a crowded Manhattan sidewalk, an acquaintance named George Trow told me that you have only to step a degree or two outside of normalcy to gain an illuminating perspective on it. Certainly that described George, who wrote for *The New Yorker* and flew as close to the sun of genius as anyone I've known. At that moment he was musing on his own predicament in life, but in the years since I have come to realize that the vantage point from my workbench is similarly askew. Furniture making, practiced as a craft in the twenty-first century, is a decidedly marginal occupation – economically, socially, technologically, and culturally. Yet it also happens to be premised on the selfsame ideal that Pirsig, Sennett, and Crawford each end up prescribing. For all of them, the key to a good life is the engaged pursuit of quality. As a craftsman I have the opportunity to turn that key every day, whether or not I actually do. The yardstick of quality is always in plain sight at the workbench.

While craft may be a byway of contemporary culture, its divergence offers a revealing prospect onto the main thoroughfare. The view from my workbench is complementary to those of Pirsig, Sennett, and Crawford. Our core difference is the role that we assign to creativity. Where they pay it little attention, my experience has been that the effort to bring something new and meaningful into the world – whether in the arts, the kitchen, or the marketplace – is exactly what generates the sense of meaning and fulfillment for which so many of us yearn so deeply. The dedication to quality that they prescribe is essential to productive creative engagement, but it is only a component, not the effort itself.

Craft is just one arena for creativity, but it is the one I know intimately. My intuition from the day I first picked up a hammer was that making things with a commitment to quality would lead to a good life. What I propose here is to retrace my steps with reference to larger frameworks – historical, sociological, psychological, and biological – to discover how and why that intuition turned out to be valid. What is it about creative work, and craft, in particular, that makes them so rewarding? What are the natures of those rewards? What, as Sennett asks, does the process of making things reveal to us about ourselves? As a furniture maker attempting to draw upon his own experience to illuminate such universal questions, I confess in advance to an ingrained pragmatism. The answers that make sense to me tend to be firmly rooted in the loam and muck of the world as I have found it, and that is where I'll begin.

CHAPTER 2

Hammering Out a Vocation

I WAS BORN IN 1951 and lived out my childhood in Rydal, an afflu-
ent suburb of Philadelphia. My father was a gregarious, capable lawyer who commuted into the city by train. My mother went back to
college to complete her undergraduate studies when my sister and I
were still quite young, and followed through to a Ph.D. in history. In a
proper autobiography there would be a significant ethnic backstory
to fill in – the cultural disparity between my father's Eastern European Jewish roots and my mother's German Jewish background, the
thrust of Reform Judaism toward assimilation, the sense of being
outsiders in an America where anti-Semitism was still evident, and
the lingering pall of the Holocaust.

But that was the world of my childhood as I understand it from
the perspective of half a century. The way it seemed to me then
was that the "Nazis" and "Japs" had been soundly defeated, the
Holocaust was ancient history like everything else that took place
before I was born, the world was fast outgrowing anti-Semitism,
and science was conquering diseases so fast that all of them would
be vanquished before my generation was old enough to be vulnerable. I grew up swaddled in the belief that tragedy was over,
that wars, persecution, and disease belonged to the past, and that,
while bad things might happen to people in books and in other
places (such as those starving children in India for whom we

ate everything on our plates), they did not happen in the world I inhabited.

There was a day when, as a small boy, I found a day-bed mattress at the top of the stairs. With great effort I maneuvered it off the landing until it started to descend the green carpeted steps on its own. I hadn't thought any further ahead than that moment, and delight flashed to fear as the mattress rapidly gained momentum and, abruptly, punched a hole in the wall opposite the bottom landing. Then – amazing! – broken chunks of granular white plaster, jagged splinters of rough wood lathe, and, most impressive of all, a dry, empty cavity behind the wall, a secret world. It had never occurred to me that there might be anything behind the painted surface. This was my mental state growing up: life was all surface. The discovery of depth, when it came during my college years, did not have the drama of a mattress smashing through a wall. Rather, a capacity for reflection seemed to emerge as gradually and fitfully as a child learns to walk.

One of the first tiny steps occurred the summer before my senior year at Germantown Friends School, when I participated in an American Friends Service Committee work camp in Owatonna, Minnesota. Our group of student volunteers lived in a bat-infested barn housing a Salvation Army store in one corner of the ground floor. It was 1968 and three of us were fledgling hippies who hung out together. There was Larry, with whom I would laugh until we collapsed to the floor, and Fred, who was moody, ironic, and intense as a Janis Ian song. What I found particularly incomprehensible about Fred was that he was in analysis. I wasn't unfamiliar with Freud, but I simply couldn't imagine what Fred found to be so miserable about. And, while I remained mystified, the simple fact of Fred, and his disdain for my own reflexive cheerfulness, was a chink in the smooth surface of life. Now I knew there was a cavity behind the wall, even if I didn't have a clue what might be inside.

Three summers later, my nineteen-year-old self lay sprawled on a bed, reading a book on social activism. Not that I had become a committed social activist – I was a college student working as a gardener on Nantucket. An antiwar, longhaired, pot-smoking, pro–civil rights student who had marched on Washington and been tear-gassed at Fort Dix for peace and justice, but a self-absorbed student nonetheless. That summer, the full extent of my daily activism consisted of choosing the colored elastic with which I would tie back my ponytail. Black symbolized Bakunin and anarchy, red was for Trotsky and socialism, blue matched my eyes.

The name of the book I was reading is lost to memory, but the gist of its message was that working to improve people's material circumstances isn't enough. Even if you manage to relieve their hunger and physical discomfort, you will not have touched their spiritual needs, which are what really matter. Better to be hungry and cold, but spiritually nourished, than to feast by a blazing hearth with spiritual emptiness gnawing away from inside.

Although I strongly suspected that no starving person would agree with the author's contention, I detected a certain truth in his words. Having attended a Quaker secondary school, I had seen many generous people – teachers, social workers, philanthropists, psychologists, Peace Corps volunteers, political activists – trying to help others through life's difficulties. Unfortunately, to my young eyes, the helpers didn't appear to be particularly happy or fulfilled themselves. There had to be more to life. The phrase "Physician, heal thyself!" came to mind, and it occurred to me that I should find out how to live my own life well before I presumed to help others. If I had to date my journey into craft, this was the moment it began.

A year later, having spent the summer in Mexico learning Spanish, I moved to Nantucket Island in search of "real life." My intent was to earn the remainder of my college credits through independent study. I didn't know what real life was. I just knew that in school I seemed to be experiencing life secondhand.

Nantucket was not then the wealthy enclave it is now; the ghosts of the nineteenth century were still in possession – and I mean this fairly literally. The Nantucket I knew as a child, starting with family vacations in the 1950s, was an isolated backwater of deteriorating old houses furnished with the hundred-year-old salvage of the island's whaling heyday. At the time I moved there, in 1972, there were only three thousand year-round residents, almost all of whom were island-born except for fifty or sixty hippie immigrants like myself. A mild collision of cultures ensued that one could stereotype as hippie-meets-redneck, but it was not particularly antagonistic. For a twenty-year-old it was a magical time and place.

I arrived on the island with three years of college behind me, a low draft number, and a box full of Marvel comic books. The low draft number argued for staying in college at the University of Pennsylvania. When my student deferment ran out, I intended to serve time in jail as a conscientious objector rather than report to basic training. The box full of comic books was research material for one of the three independent study courses I took that fall – a sociological evaluation of comic-book readership through story content, graphics, and advertisements.

But what I really did that fall was begin my own life, to the extent that one can while one's father (my parents now being divorced) is still paying the rent. I was free to do what I wanted, when I wanted, as long as I wrote those papers. Admittedly, what I wanted to do was pretty simple stuff. Walks over the moors. Walks on the beaches. Walks through town. Pick rose hips and plums and grapes as each came in season and learn to make jelly. Cook pies and stir-fries and bake bread. And, every evening, get stoned with my buddy Al and listen to Incredible String Band records for hours on end.

In December, I sealed my final term paper into a manila envelope and dropped it in the mail. I had accumulated enough credits to graduate, so right before Christmas I started looking for a job. A temporary job, since it couldn't be more than a few months until a summons arrived from the draft board in Philadelphia.

I had no specific career ambitions, although it was now time to earn a living. What I did have was the desire to discover a better way to live than my parents' generation appeared to have found. In this I was very much a representative of my own generation. We grew up in a prosperous, postwar America where, despite every sign of worldly success, adult life looked shallow and, in the twin shadows of the Vietnam War and the civil rights movement, morally bankrupt. Today we would use the word *unfulfilled* instead of *shallow*, but the concept of fulfillment as a life goal was not current in the sixties. Our parents were children of the Great Depression. For them, the bottom-line measure was economic security. In any case, I looked at the grown-up world and said, All this for what? My life and those of many of my contemporaries may be seen as attempts to answer that question – not theoretically, but in practice.

The search for a good life was not the relatively simple matter of getting from point A to point B over difficult terrain (which better describes the path to success in an established profession like medicine or law). It was more like being a fifteenth-century European explorer navigating with maps on which a known, finely detailed world is bordered by sketchy depictions of legendary continents and fabled cities – a voyage over uncharted seas to find out what really lay beyond.

We were all looking for accurate maps of the world, my friends and I. My best friend from high school, Scott, was studying Buddhism under Chögyam Trungpa Rinpoche. A close friend from college, Tom, was learning to organize strikes and boycotts under Cesar Chavez. I was too skeptical of gurus, politics, and office work to journey alongside either one. Thinking of this now, a Jackson Browne lyric of that era comes to mind: "Together we went traveling, as we received the call / His destination India, and I had none at all."

Although I may not have known where I was going, I had at least figured out that the work I chose would continue to shape me, so I knew I had to choose carefully. Obvious as that may seem today, at the time it was a major realization. I grew up in a world where, as characterized by physician and author Abigail Zuger, "the adult brain was considered an immutable machine, as wonderfully precise as a clock in a locked case. Every part had a specific purpose, none could be replaced or repaired, and the machine was destined to tick in unchanging rhythm until its gears corroded with age."[3] As a child I had assumed that the process of growing up ended when you finished college, after which you stayed the same person for the rest of your life. Only as I approached adulthood did I realize that life is a process of continual becoming.

Carpentry

The work I chose turned out to be the work that chose me. The first person to offer me a job that December was a carpenter. He might just as easily have been a plumber or an electrician, since building trades were prevalent on Nantucket.

Carpentry was new to me, and that first job was not a promising start. We were a young three-man crew left to hold the fort while the boss wintered in the Caribbean. The lead carpenter, Kendrick, was a West Indian who mostly thought about meeting girls with "powe'ful thighs." Neither he nor Bobby, a ruddy-faced construction worker from South Carolina, knew enough to make us productive. There were days when we only managed to fit one rake board to a gable between the three of us, all the while freezing our asses off (as we put it) in the February cold.

My father wasn't happy with my choice of work. He'd always assumed I'd pursue a professional career such as law, medicine, or even, God forbid, architecture. He wasn't prepared for his son to become a tradesman. More than once he said, "You'll regret doing work that doesn't challenge your mind." But from the start there was a mind/body wholeness to carpentry that put it way ahead of what I imagined office work to be. Nonetheless, I did make time that winter, while my brain was still tracking in an academic groove, to take the law school admission test, just in case my father turned out to be right. My mother, on the other hand, was fully supportive. If I had chosen to rob banks for a living she would have been proud, so long as I did it well.

Skilled labor was completely new to me. Back in high school my father had given me the nickname Helpful Henry after I dropped and shattered a light bulb while changing a ceiling fixture in the kitchen. That nickname, with its implication of ineptitude, was mine to inhabit or not, and I didn't really want it. I see it now as my father's projection of his own disinterest in mechanical matters. He couldn't have pointed to the carburetor under the hood of his Pontiac LeMans and he didn't care. In the Jewish-American culture in which my father grew up, working with your hands dropped you many rungs down the social ladder. Yet carpentry provided an identity into which I was eager to grow. The carpenters I knew on Nantucket were young off-islanders who, like me, had moved there to find a different sort of life. They were independent, irreverent, competent, and self-reliant. I couldn't wait for the day when the soft leather of my new hammer holster would be as scarred and weathered as theirs.

In taking a job as a carpenter I was challenging elements of a story I had inherited from my parents and their parents before them about who I was and how the world worked. But I was not a lone rebel. The ideas I was trying out permeated the culture of the time like spores of wild yeast. The process of rewriting the story by which I found my place in the world was simultaneously both personal and generational.

Carl Borchert

In January 1973, the Vietnam War ended and Secretary of Defense Melvin Laird announced the end of the draft. For an apprentice carpenter who had been expecting a draft notice any day, the world became more luminous. I no longer faced an imminent detour to Vietnam or prison.

Then, in March, I was offered a job on a more dynamic carpentry crew. My new employer, Carl Borchert, had worked as an engineer outside of Boston, designing weapon systems for Raytheon, before moving his young family to Nantucket to build a more morally attuned life. Carl was six foot six, full-bearded, and Abraham-Lincoln thin. The one time I saw him trip and fall, he went over with the slow-motion grandeur of a redwood.

Carl's thinness was deceptive, though. One Saturday afternoon, my friend Al slid my 1967 Toyota Corolla off one of the dirt roads that crisscross the open moors of Nantucket. The rear passenger wheel hung in the air about five feet above a cranberry bog, and we exited the driver's side quite gingerly so as not to tip the car over the embankment. In those days a Toyota was not much more substantial than a tin can with a windshield, and Al and I were strong young carpenters, but we couldn't budge the car by lifting the rear bumper. So we walked to the Polpis Road and hitched into town to find Carl, confident he could solve any practical problem. To our surprise, instead of hooking up a winch or a towrope, Carl simply stood in the bog, hefted the Toyota onto his shoulder, and shifted it back onto solid earth, easy as pie.

I worked for Carl about a year and a half, building vacation houses from the ground up. He was not an easy boss, but he ran a cheerful, motivated crew, and I learned a tremendous amount. The other carpenters were Billy, a red-haired stoner and early EST cultee[4]; Dave, a scruffy Boston tough whose idea of a joke was "What do Germans like to do at the beach? Fry kikes and shoot Segals!"; and Joe, a family man who was so tightly wound that he wouldn't pick up female hitchhikers on placid Nantucket Island for fear of being accused of rape.

Being fresh out of school, I was accustomed to frequent feedback. Good grades mattered. But Carl wasn't one to praise, although he assuredly let me know when my work wasn't up to standard. One day, I was hammering vinyl-clad windows in place, missed a nail, and cracked the vinyl. A few minutes later, try as I might, I made the same mistake again. That was when Carl added the growled phrase "numb nuts" to my growing carpentry lexicon. It was several months before I figured out that Carl's signature on my paycheck was the full measure of his approval – the only one I was likely to see and the only one that really mattered. I had graduated into the working world.

For all that, Carl Borchert had a nature as true as a granite block. You knew upon meeting him that the rough, honest surface carried right through to the core – that he possessed a reliable moral compass. I don't mean by this that he was absorbed in a deep inner conversation or was self-righteous. His morality found expression in the integrity of his actions. As a builder, for example, he didn't do the fanciest work, but every step in the process was done solidly, soundly, with no corners cut. And just as he chose carpentry over weapons, so Carl eventually chose restoration over new construction. He didn't want to contribute to the overbuilding of Nantucket as it became clear that the lovely, quiet, open-spaced island that he loved was doomed to overdevelopment.

The house that Carl built for his family, a pole barn, was a metaphor for the man. No plasterboard interior, no trim, no finish. The aesthetic of the inside was formed by the exterior and structural components. Telephone poles, redolent of creosote, ran floor to ceiling at wide intervals. Between them, the interior walls were formed by the backside of tongue-and-groove exterior sheathing. Looking up to the ceiling, one saw the underside of second-story pine floor-boards, framed between floor joists.

When I picture that house now, I see late-afternoon sunlight streaming through the west-facing kitchen window. A small vase of yellow and purple wildflowers, translucent in the raking light, sits on the worn maple table. Kitchen paraphernalia and books crowd the unfinished pine shelves on the wall opposite. A tacked-up post-card shows a large, bearded man standing at a sink piled comically high with dishes, with a caption that reads, "Because a man's got to do what a man's got to do." The only building in sight is a small barn down across the meadow, where Carl and his wife, Karen, keep horses, goats, and chickens. By the barn is an extensive vegetable garden, fenced to keep the deer out. On the far side of the garden is a marshy expanse where wild iris bloom in spring, and beyond the marsh rises the low, scrub oak forest of Nantucket.

To the northeast, behind the house, is a major icon of my life: Carl and Karen's clothesline. Two cross-barred, gray-weathered posts rise out of the grass, with lines of sash cord strung between. It may not sound like much, but set in the mown meadow between house and wood, that clothesline possessed a simple, functional beauty that bespoke an entire way of life.

The Carpenter's Life

September of 1973 marked the beginning of my second year on Nantucket. My father, visiting, said that my newly muscled fingers looked like swollen sausages. My hands had indeed changed, and I had newfound confidence in them. On Carl's crew, I saw an entire house grow under their care. In my spare time, I bought an abandoned 1952 Ford pickup for twenty-five bucks and put it back on the road, figuring things out as I went along. Mostly I worked with parts that I surreptitiously scavenged from other abandoned vehicles, plus the occasional new item ordered by mail from J. C. Whitney. I replaced the brakes, brake cylinders, transmission, starter, and fuel pump; rebuilt the carburetor; put in new sparkplugs and distributor cables; rebuilt the bed; and much more. I spent as much time under that truck with a wrench as I did driving it. I don't know which I enjoyed more.

I had a new dog, too, Bear Boy, whom I had saved from execution at the pound when his first owner gave up on him. Bear was a slight, handsome, black Lab mix – an incorrigible mutt who couldn't have cared less about relating to humans. His only interests were fighting and fornication. When a bitch was in heat anywhere on the island, Bear would be gone for days, enthusiastically brawling with other suitors outside the domicile of his intended, until I finally received the predictable call from Linda Cahoon, the dogcatcher, telling me where to retrieve him.

I also started my first beard that September, partially to keep my face warm through the coming winter's outdoor work, partially as another step to becoming whoever I might be. So much was changing in my life – I was changing so much – that I half expected, half hoped to see a more seasoned, knowing face emerge from the cocoon of my beard the following spring.

Along with learning to tell one end of a nail from the other, I was discovering new ways to be in the world. In junior high and high school I had been the youngest in my class and slow to reach puberty; I had been small, relatively nonathletic, and occasionally bullied. I had taken refuge in being smart – or, to be more precise, in trying to be smarter than others. But as a carpenter on Nantucket I found that the competitive aspect of my personality separated me from other people. What I wanted, and what was available to me, was community. I had left college looking for real life, and now I had found it. Intuitively, I knew I was on the road to discovering what a good life might be.

First Epiphany

Fast-forward a little more than a year, to November 1974. I have fallen deeply in love and my girlfriend and I are caretaking the Heller estate, a two-hundred-year-old cape on a hundred acres of land half-way out the Hummock Pond Road. I'm still pounding nails for Carl Borchert. My hammer holster is weathered and scarred. Gail works as a cleaning lady for Mrs. Mitchell, a wealthy elderly woman whose house has been frozen in time since the moment her husband died, twenty years before. Not a frayed, monogrammed towel or a thread-bare linen sheet has been replaced.

The Hellers are in Florida for the winter. They have left two elderly, incontinent dogs in our care. Pookie is a blind German shorthaired pointer. Pepi is a deaf Weimaraner with senile dementia. Every morning before breakfast our walks to the far end of the property combine pathos with slapstick comedy. Pepi forgets we're taking a walk, drifts off, and can't hear me call. Pookie follows the other dogs until she crosses the trail of a deer, at which point she joyously chases down the scent until she runs head-first into a tree. Bear Boy picks up the trail that Pookie has started and is sometimes gone for hours. Meanwhile, back at the house, Gail washes the piss-soaked towels the old dogs use for bedding and mops the concrete floor of the laundry room where they sleep. Aside from the dogs' room, though, the old house is a special place. On cold weekend mornings I light fires in all three downstairs fireplaces and we have friends over to breakfast. After a few hours, the radiant brick hearths seem to awaken the old house to memories of earlier centuries.

Gail is an aspiring weaver. A cherry loom occupies one end of the dining room, and she has applied to Capellagården, a crafts school in Sweden. I am intent on a career designing and building houses on spec, but have applied to the school's woodworking program so that we can travel to Sweden together.

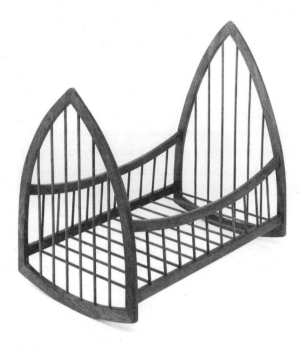

The design for this cradle, found in a book, was the author's first furniture project.

It's almost Thanksgiving, and our friends Nils and Joyce are expecting their first child at any minute. They are the first among our peers to have a child, so this is a major event, mysterious to us all. I decide to make them a cradle, thinking that I might as well get some furniture-making experience now that we've applied to school.

Next to the Heller house is a barn with a single rusty table saw in an unheated workshop. Working from a photograph in a book, I buy pine and dowels from the local lumber yard and set to work. Furniture making turns out to be considerably different from carpentry. It requires joinery: bridle joints to assemble the triangular frames that curve like Gothic arches at each end of the cradle, and mortise and tenon joints to secure the aprons that traverse the ends like a suspension bridge. It entails sensitive shaping with a rasp and file to make the wood gentle to the hand and eye. It demands a precision that reveals the slightest gap or flaw.

After three days of intense focus, cold, and solitude, the cradle is complete – a miraculous birth in its own right. I have somehow transformed benign intent into a beautiful, functional object. This is my moment on the road to Damascus. I am overtaken by a most unexpected passion. Within two months of making the cradle I will quit my carpentry job to make furniture full-time in the Heller barn. In the meantime, Gail and I will be turned down by Capellagården.

Back in 1974 one did not routinely meet furniture makers. There were few craft fairs, there was no *Fine Woodworking* magazine. In the entire nation there was only one small Woodcraft store where you could buy traditional woodworking tools such as mortise gauges, and those had to be imported from England. Out in the barn, fingers numb with cold, I could believe I was rediscovering a lost art. After the cradle I built a ladder-back chair, then started on a rocker. My meager guides were two books that I was given for Christmas by Gail and her sister. (My father gave me a drawing board and drafting equipment, although he was no happier with furniture making than he had been with carpentry.) I also had a friend, Jon, who had spent a few months sanding for a woodworker in New Jersey. Between us, we could usually figure out the sequence of steps for a given project.

As my woodworking horizons slowly expanded, I designed each new project around whatever technique I wanted to learn next. My goal was to become a proficient craftsman; design was a secondary consideration. So began a decade during which the challenges of furniture making consumed me. While my friends would talk and listen to music at a bar, I'd sit there sketching chairs on napkins. I gave little thought to practicalities such as income. I simply inhabited my passion.

CHAPTER 3

The Seductive Ideology of Craft

MY ENTRY INTO CRAFT was an intensely singular experience. But whether I was rinsing mung bean sprouts in the kitchen sink with Joni Mitchell's captivating soprano on the stereo or out in the barn shaping the arm of a red oak rocking chair with a coarse Nicholson rasp, I was very much a product of the historical moment. It was no accident that a young person in 1974 was searching for a meaningful and fulfilling way to inhabit adulthood, nor that he would turn to craft. The culture of my time and place poured through me like water through a weir. Craft was a concept that lodged in the netting.

In furniture making, beginnings are critical. For a simple frame-and-panel cabinet door to stay flat over the long haul, and not become too tight in summer or overly gapped in winter, success starts with the choice of timber. Not just what species or which plank, but also from which part of the board one saws the stiles and rails, how dry the wood is, the method by which it was dried, and how it was stored and handled. All this before the actual work of milling the timber flat and square, laying out and cutting the joinery, making and fitting the panel, assembling, trimming, fitting, hinging, latching, and finishing. Throughout the entire process, the quality achievable at each stage is utterly dependent on the care with which the craftsman has accomplished every previous step.

Likewise, as someone trying to write about the nature and rewards of craft, it seems important to construct a sound foundation by being precise early on about what I mean by *craft*. The word is a chameleon. It is both verb and noun. It is used to impute quality to everything from one-of-a-kind handmade objects to mass-produced industrial products. It is closely linked to equally amorphous off-shoots such as *craftsman, craftsmanship,* and the less gracious *crafter*. A lawyer may be said to craft an agreement with all the grammatical correctness with which a potter is said to craft a teacup. An actor practices his[5] craft on the stage as readily as a blacksmith practices his at the forge. There is high craft, low craft, reproduction craft, and conceptual craft. There is craft in legacy materials such as wood, clay, fiber, metal, and glass, and there is anything-goes craft made with plastic, concrete, and duct tape.

Specifically, I am writing about craft as it is practiced today by professionals and amateurs throughout the United States, Europe, Japan, and other industrialized nations – countries where manufac-tured goods have almost entirely supplanted handmade products in meeting the material needs of society. In these countries, contempo-rary craft items stand in sharp contrast to preindustrial objects that we also designate as craft. Premodern craft was made to satisfy cul-turally prescribed, functional purposes. A hatbox held a hat, a snuff box held snuff, a clothes press held clothes. Contemporary craft, being economically marginal, is created primarily to address the spiritual needs of its *maker*. As a result, it often lacks utility and its practical disposition may be left to the whim of the purchaser. Wan-dering the aisles of a craft show today, you are likely to find everything from sturdy, utilitarian coffee tables to abstract wall decorations, with the middle ground occupied by chairs that are too angular for comfort, teapots that drip, and jewelry that threatens bodily harm to the wearer. This is not a criticism of nonutilitarian craft. Dysfunc-tion, handled competently, generates significant emotional power.

It would be a pleasure to offer a concise definition of craft. People often assume it is either a timeless category of human endeavor (such as religion and marriage) or of manmade objects (such as tools and dwellings). But when it comes to definition, craft is a moving target. Like its cousins art and design, craft is a cultural construct that evolves in response to changing mindsets and conditions of society.

In fact, the concept of craft as we know it is a recent invention. Weavers and potters in the Middle Ages, woodworkers and goldsmiths during the Renaissance; cabinetmakers employed by Louis XV in the Age of Enlightenment – none of these practitioners thought of their work as craft. Henry Wadsworth Longfellow did not think his village blacksmith was practicing a craft in 1840, when he placed the fellow's forge under a spreading chestnut tree. Our contemporary notion of craft, whether as a form of production or a type of object, originated with the flowering of the Arts and Crafts Movement in Britain, a mere 130 years ago.

Prior to the Arts and Crafts Movement, the English word *craft* was used predominantly to indicate a capacity for shrewdness and manipulation. (Think of coinages such as *witchcraft* and *statecraft*.[6]) Then, in the turbulent wake of the Industrial Revolution, *craft* was given new meaning by the founders of the emerging Arts and Crafts Movement. Foremost among them were John Ruskin (1819–1900) and William Morris (1834–1896). These early socialists took three strands of nineteenth-century thought – the applied (or decorative) arts, the vernacular, and the politics of work – and wove them into a single, compelling, counter-industrial narrative that they labeled *craft*.[7] Fifty-plus years later, that narrative would powerfully inform the rise of the studio craft movement, my craft movement.

The best way to understand craft, I believe, is to think of it as a conversation flowing through time. Or, more precisely, as a recent eddy in a broad conversation about object-making that began at least 2.5 million years ago, when our hominid ancestors were making tools in the Olduvai Gorge, in Tanzania. Since then, the making of tools and objects has progressed to increasingly effective techniques, endlessly more inventive forms, and fantastically elaborate functions – from the chipped chert axes of the Stone Age to the flying stone buttresses of Notre Dame, the Indiana limestone–clad Empire State Building, and the silicon computer chips in the machine at my fingertips. The increase in sophistication has not resulted from any biological evolution of our species; instead, it illustrates the evolution of culture. Knowledge gained through experience has accreted from generation to generation (along with beliefs, values, and aesthetic ideals), passed on by example and explanation. This flow of information through millennia is the conversation of object making. We participate in it every time we make an object and, to a lesser extent, every time we interact with one.

When I began to make furniture in November of 1974, I was working in a partial vacuum. The craft of furniture making had been largely eradicated by industrialization. Like many woodworkers of my generation, I was on my own, feeling my way in the dark. Nonetheless, long before I picked up my first chisel I had spent my youth being informed by the built environment. I had internalized a rich vocabulary of materials, forms, functions, proportions, and emotional associations that strongly influenced what I would choose to make and why I chose to make it. And when I did finally grasp a chisel, I became the instant beneficiary of countless generations of accumulated experience in tool design and metallurgy.

That Christmas of 1974, my first woodworking books – Charles Hayward's *Woodwork Joints* and Rafael Teller's *Woodwork* – brought me deeper into the conversation of furniture making. But more profoundly, my hands began to discover the nature of tools and materials for themselves. Naturally, it wasn't long before I started to hold up my end of the discussion. Sharing sharpening tips with a carpenter friend, or displaying a rocking chair in a gallery, I began to actively inform other people's ideas about objects and making.

Over ensuing decades there would be an explosion of communication among neophyte woodworkers like myself. *Fine Woodworking* magazine began publication in 1975 and was soon joined by a half dozen similar publications. Through their pages – and books that would be published, schools that would be founded, crafts shows that would proliferate, and galleries that would open – we became what is now called an open-source community. A brief trip through the *Fine Woodworking* collection in our school library graphically illustrates the rising tide of refinement. Within a generation we had bootstrapped our collective skills to a level of knowledge and proficiency that arguably surpassed that of the eighteenth-century French and German *ébénistes* whose secrets we had presumed lost forever.

The conversation of object making has coursed through the emergence and decline of civilizations. New voices have interrupted it, new technologies have influenced it, and changing economic and political circumstances have reoriented it, but the conversation never abates. The currents we label craft, art, and design entered only yesterday in the time scale of history. As they evolve and, eventually, dissipate, the conversation will no doubt continue undiminished, for we are an object-making species.

The Axioms of Craft

When I was seduced by woodworking in my early twenties, I had never, to my knowledge, met a craftsman. Furniture makers, potters, glassblowers, smiths, weavers, bookbinders, and all their kind were thin on the ground. Then, when I was finally introduced to a skilled furniture restorer, on Nantucket, I couldn't credit him as the real thing. He was a defeated alcoholic whose life was a shambles. In no way did he match up to the Hallmark-card image of the craftsman I carried in my head. I had never consciously thought about it, but I expected a *real* craftsman to be a skilled tradesman, secure in the knowledge of his hands and the strength of his character, calm at his workbench, pursuing a simple, peaceful life in idyllic surroundings. More like Carl Borchert, had he built furniture instead of houses.

Where did that burnished image come from? It was a direct legacy of the Arts and Crafts Movement, a distillation of the three main ingredients – the applied arts, the vernacular, and the politics of work – from which the ideologues of the movement had concocted the idea of craft.

Right through the late Middle Ages there had been no historical distinction between fine and applied arts. Sculptors belonged to the same guilds as stone masons; painters associated with gilders and saddlers. All of their trades were accorded relatively equal merit. Only when the Renaissance began to elevate the life of the mind above the life of the body, approximately six hundred years ago, did hierarchical distinctions begin to emerge.[8] The imposing rampart between the fine and applied arts that Ruskin and Morris confronted (and that many contemporary craftspeople continue to assault or lament) was long in the making. Three hundred years after da Vinci painted the *Mona Lisa*, the Enlightenment finally provided strong enough mortar. This was the philosophy of Cartesian dualism, which formally divided mind and matter into separate and unequal camps. Art happily snuggled into the category of mind, while all other types of object making were associated with the body, branded as "applied arts," and banished to lesser estates.

The concept of the vernacular was a nineteenth-century invention, a reaction to the social dislocation of the Industrial Revolution. It surfaced as a nostalgia for objects and customs that appeared to have risen directly out of folk tradition, untainted by the artificiality, venality, or complexity of contemporary life. Within the Arts and Crafts Movement, it led to an idealization of rural, handmade production. Today, the notion of the vernacular remains firmly entrenched. I don't consider myself to be particularly sentimental, for example, but when I see a wooden pitchfork with graceful steam-bent tines, a birch-bark canoe, or a centuries-worn Windsor chair, I can't help but read it as a message from a simpler, more poetic age.

The third strand in Ruskin and Morris's concept of craft, the politics of work, was inherent to nineteenth-century political philosophy. Primary concerns were the nature of work, the moral welfare of the worker, the health of society, and the causal connections among them. Karl Marx (1818–1883) was the most famous theorist to travel this road, but others included Thomas Carlyle (1795–1881) and Thorstein Veblen (1857–1929). Ruskin famously wrote about the "degradation of the operative into a machine" in *The Stones of Venice*, where he went on to say:

> It is not that men are ill fed, but that they have no pleasure in the work by which they make their bread, and therefore look to wealth as the only means of pleasure. It is not that men are pained by the scorn of the upper classes, but they cannot endure their own; for they feel that the kind of labour to which they are condemned is verily a degrading one, and makes them less than men.[9]

Ruskin and Morris welded the ideas of the applied arts, the vernacular, and the politics of work into a theory of production intended to counteract the evils of industrial capitalism. Their craft worker would make objects of aesthetic merit from start to finish in salubrious surroundings, with personal responsibility for quality. Such improved conditions of labor would promote psychological health and produce better citizens.

As it turned out, though, the Arts and Crafts Movement never realized its ambition to transform society. It foundered on two rocks. One was financial: The workshops set up by Morris and others could only succeed by creating fashionable consumer goods for the wealthy few. Work organized along the lines of craft simply could not compete economically with mass production. The other was the cataclysm of the First World War, which transformed the cultural landscape in ways that made the concerns of the movement seem irrelevant.

The Arts and Crafts Movement failed to deflect the juggernaut of industrialization in any noticeable way – either in regard to means of production or conditions of labor. Nonetheless, it left a lasting imprint on the conversations of design and object making. The aesthetic ideas of Ruskin and Morris would influence the Bauhaus in Germany, de Stijl in the Netherlands, art nouveau in France, the Wiener Werkstätte in Austria, and Frank Lloyd Wright's Prairie School of architecture in the U.S., among other notable manifestations.

The ideology of craft continued to inform the conversation of object making throughout the twentieth century. It shaped the ways in which people thought about what should be made, who should make it, how it should be made, and why it was made. Although the Arts and Crafts Movement petered out, the discussion it inaugurated continued to reverberate, until finally the concept of craft so permeated the public mind that the making of most non-art, non-manufactured objects throughout history came to be called craft in retrospect. Certainly, for my generation of craftsmen, the theories of Ruskin and Morris were pivotal, whether or not we had ever heard mention of their names.

CHAPTER 4

Live from New York

WHEN I PICKED UP a hammer right out of college, I discovered that skilled manual work offered spiritual rewards to which academic institutions and my parent's social milieu were oblivious. My subsequent decision to quit carpentry for furniture making turned out to be equally fateful, although at the time I intuited the difference between the two occupations more than I rationally understood it. As a carpenter I had worked with my hands. As a furniture maker I began to work creatively with my hands, which has made all the difference. Becoming a carpenter may have been a process of self-definition and self-transformation, but as I gained competence the daily work of carpentry became a known quantity. Designing and building furniture, on the other hand, has never lost the challenge of exploration and the delight of discovery. While it is possible to calcify in a creative field – to stop asking new questions and stick with what one knows – by its very nature furniture making offers doors to new experience at every turn.

As a young carpenter, I found ready employment and I had a role model in Carl Borchert, whose integrity and independence provided signposts to a good life. As a nascent craftsman in a society where the trade of furniture making had apparently vanished, I was going to have to find my way on my own. The first step would be to make the transition from wanting to become a craftsman to actually being one.

Frederick, Maryland

In June of 1975, a year and a half after I made my first cradle, I packed a truckload of handmade furniture into a well-worn Ford Econoline van that had succeeded my pickup truck, boarded a ferry from Nantucket to Woods Hole, and drove to Frederick, Maryland, to participate in my first major craft show. I had no idea what to expect. What I found were scores of young craftspeople setting up a nomadic encampment that was a cross between Woodstock and a medieval market fair. Craft shows were highly informal events in those days, often as not held in livestock barns on county fairgrounds. I didn't sell more than a few small boxes, but it was affirming to have people connect to my work.

I was single again (my own damn fault) and had spent the past winter aching over Gail in a claustrophobic house on a dirt road about two miles outside of town. My workshop was down in the tiny, windowless basement, where I had to duck floor joists every time I moved. I don't remember everything I made in the course of those ten months, but they included an oak cabinet for a tugboat someone was converting into a yacht, heart-shaped mahogany boxes for Valentine's Day, a walnut quilt rack, a set of carved walnut boxes that a customer characterized as "canary coffins," and a run of six cherry rocking chairs. I was hugely ignorant – I barely had a clue how to sharpen a chisel and would pretty much hack away at wood with a hand plane – but lovely objects still took shape under my hands. Looking back, it amazes me.

On the morning I left for Frederick, Bear Boy was strangely apathetic. I had to lift him into the passenger seat of the van. By the time we reached New York City he could barely walk. I took him to the Animal Medical Center and two days later learned over the telephone, from Frederick, that he had lymphoma. The next day I called back to discuss treatment and was told that he had died overnight.

When I returned home after a week off-island, I was ready to leave Nantucket for good. Heartbreak over Gail was one reason, the absence of Bear another, plus I didn't want to be there for the tidal wave of real estate development that even then was looming on the horizon. Mostly, though, I was ambitious to be a furniture maker, and the craft show had made it clear that living on the mainland offered more opportunities to learn and to sell. The amiable search for a good life that I had embarked upon five years earlier had been hijacked by a passion for furniture making that drove me forward with its own logic. I was becoming aware that a good life was not some Shangri-La waiting to be stumbled upon. One constructed it from the materials at hand.

Frederick Again

Having decided to leave Nantucket, I arbitrarily settled upon Washington D.C. as my next home. But the only house I found that met my three requirements – inexpensive rent, space for a workshop, and sufficient distance from neighbors that the sound of a table saw wouldn't bother anyone – was forty miles to the west in Frederick, Maryland. So to Frederick I returned.

The subsequent year in Frederick was one of semi-monastic isolation. All I did, Monday through Saturday, was make furniture in a one-car garage under the house. In particular, I recall a drop-leaf walnut table, a cherry trestle desk, a red oak bed with a pattern of hearts sawn out of the headboard, and a sculptural music stand. I gained confidence. My work was shown in galleries in New Jersey and Washington. I was written up in the *Washington Star*. A senator

invited me to see Jefferson's writing desk at the State Department
prior to ordering a small writing desk of his own.

I didn't know a soul in Frederick. There were weeks when the
full extent of my personal human interaction consisted of thank-
ing the cashier at the supermarket. The telephone rarely rang, and
when it did I would limber up my croaky voice with practice hellos
before lifting the receiver. Eventually, I began to talk to my table saw.
Not full-blown conversations – I wasn't crazy – just the occasional
companionable observation. In the evenings, having no television,
I sometimes entertained myself by making funny faces in the bathroom mirror.

The exception to my isolation came every Saturday, when I drove
forty-five minutes to spend the night with my Uncle Ed and Aunt
Mickey in Bethesda. We would eat dinner and talk and then, on Sunday, walk the Chesapeake & Ohio Canal path beside the Potomac
River and talk. Sunday evening before I left, we would watch Master-
piece Theater on television and talk. It didn't matter much what we
talked about; it was the pleasure of sharp conversation that counted.
At dinner, I would often haul their dictionary or encyclopedia to the
table to settle any disputes.

I watched the mailbox in front of the house in Frederick as expec-
tantly as a Melanesian might have scanned the sky for manna in the
days of the cargo cults. But furniture orders never materialized. Nor
was there any reason they should have. I didn't have a clue about
marketing and somehow assumed that the world would find me,
unprompted. The brown rice jar became my financial barometer.
When it fell to a five-day supply I would telephone my father for a
check, for which I was both grateful and ashamed. It was, in retrospect, a stark and solitary year. I was achingly lonely, anxious about
money, and insecure in so many ways, yet I had no complaints. I was
deeply engaged in acquiring the skills of craftsmanship; my days in
the garage workshop were full. By the end of the year in Frederick

I had made the transition from wanting to be a furniture maker to thinking of myself as a furniture maker.

New York

In August 1977 I moved to New York City so I could learn drafting and drawing by taking night courses at the now-defunct Jiranek School of Furniture Design and Technology. By day, after considerable looking, I set up my workshop in a relatively inexpensive storefront on Elizabeth Street in Little Italy, between Houston and Prince, a block off the Bowery (plate 1).

Elizabeth Street was awash in the city's demographic tides. There were elderly Italians whose children had long since moved out to more upscale boroughs and suburbs, lively Dominican families who dominated street life, reserved Chinese pushing north from Chinatown, and hopeful young artists living at the edge of Soho, which was just starting to percolate as an arts district. The few storefront businesses on the block were still Italian-owned: Mary's butcher shop next door, Mike's hardware store across the street, the sandwich shop down at the corner of Prince where I first tasted an eggplant parmesan sub, and a dry-cleaner's that was rumored to be a Mafia front.

The day I moved in was sweltering. Across the street, just to the left of the hardware store, children were playing around a jet of water from a yellow hydrant that thrummed a tattoo against the side of every passing vehicle. Having read numerous subway posters warning that open hydrants reduce water pressure for fighting fires, I strode across the street with a heavy, orange Stillson wrench and shut off the hydrant. I couldn't have made more impact if I had cartwheeled down the street naked. Children and adults stared in disbelief. I should have been branded an outcast then and there, but what happened, I suspect, was that Mike, who was sitting on a lawn chair in front of his hardware store, took bemused pity on my obvious lack of survival instincts. Over the next two years there were subtle indications that he had placed me under his protection. When someone smashed a neighboring store's plate glass windows, Mike assured me I didn't have to worry about my own.

I certainly had little understanding of the environment into which I had plunged. There didn't seem to be any crime on my block, but it never occurred to me to wonder why. Then, when I had been there a year or so, a young derelict who had wandered over from the Bowery foolishly snatched a purse from one of the elderly Italian women who congregated at Mary's butcher shop. He didn't make it thirty yards before knives and guns appeared everywhere and he was knocked down to the concrete, kicked and beaten like an errant mutt, jerked to his feet, and roughly escorted off the block. It was only then that I realized that the Dominican and Italian men on the block carried concealed weapons. It was their family neighborhood, and they kept it safe.

My rundown storefront was small, perhaps 400 square feet. I restored the plate glass windows, repaired and painted the exterior, and partitioned the inside to create a showroom at the front and a workshop at the rear. It was a proud moment when I hung out my first sign: "Peter Korn: Fine Furniture."

Finding a place to live was my next priority. At first I stayed with two sisters I knew from Nantucket who shared a loft apartment off Gramercy Park. Then, for several months, I rented a dingy fifth-floor walkup on Prince Street, around the corner from my workshop. The building was a warren of Italian families who seemed to have been there for decades. When the plumbing backed up and loose tea leaves began to bubble out of sink drains on the first floor, everyone immediately knew whom to blame; I was the only possible tea drinker in the entire building. Finally, I ended up three doors down from my workshop, in a second-floor apartment that had two

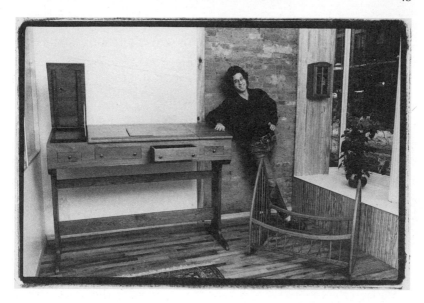

The author in his workshop showroom at 236 Elizabeth Street in New York, 1978.

special features: a bathtub under the kitchen counter and a tribe of albino cockroaches in the cupboard.

After the isolation of Frederick, New York was a social whirl. I'd make furniture all day, as I had before, but being in a storefront, people would stop in all the time – neighborhood artists, potential customers, and visiting friends. Many afternoons I would put a closed sign on the door and walk with a friend down to Café Roma, on Broome Street, for cappuccino and *sfogliatelle*.

I sketched every day in a spiral-bound notebook, sometimes designing on commission, but more often developing speculative pieces to sell at craft shows and through my showroom. The entire process of making furniture was captivating. First I would tease an idea into being with pencil and paper, sketching and drafting to think through the challenges of construction, wood movement, joinery, proportion, function, and a dozen other factors. Then I would ride

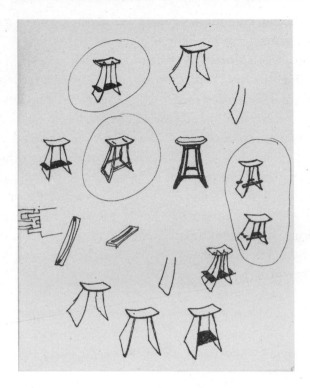

Page from the author's sketchbook.

the subway out to Rosenzweig Lumber in the Bronx to sort through
bays of dusty, rough-sawn hardwood for the few boards that had the
best grain, width, and color. A day or two later Rosenzweig's delivery truck would block our narrow street and I would start the real
work: marking out rough cuts with a framing square, straight edge,
and lumber crayon; milling the components flat and square with the
band saw, jointer, planer, and table saw; hand-planing boards that
were too wide for my jointer; cutting dovetails and mortise and ten-
ons with marking gauges, a sliding T-bevel, a try square, chisels, a
coping saw, and a back saw; smoothing surfaces with a scraper and
sandpaper; gluing up with clamps; trimming proud joints with a

block plane; and, after more scraping and sanding, applying a tung oil finish that finally unveiled the beauty of the wood.

Every day was a process of learning and becoming. When I hung out my shingle in New York, I had been making furniture for only three years and was entirely self-taught. The extent of my ignorance might have been crushing had I been fully aware of it. But the world made room for my modest skills. The major craft show in the country at the time was held in Rhinebeck, New York, by the American Craft Council, and I believe that in 1978 I was one of only six full-time furniture makers out of five hundred exhibitors. In the entire country there were relatively few independent woodworkers building furniture one piece at a time from their own designs, and many of them didn't know much more than I did. We were all scaling the steep front end of the learning curve.

It was not just *making* furniture that I loved, but also *being* a furniture maker. I liked being self-employed, working hard to meet my personal standards, and trusting in the skill and strength of my hands. Having a storefront location meant having a public presence. Mary the butcher, Mike across the street, the Dominicans who frequented the social club two doors down, and the local artists all knew me first and foremost as a furniture maker. My friends from high school, college, and Nantucket now thought of me as a furniture maker. I had traveled far from the world of my parents, and also a long way from the career expectations implicit in a first-class education at Germantown Friends and Penn.

I made a lot of furniture during my two years in New York. A dining table, occasional chairs, a bed, coffee tables, benches, rocking chairs, music stands, desks, jewelry boxes, a cradle, a room-divider screen, a wall cabinet, and more. Although it was still a financial struggle, I was standing on my own two feet. I no longer had to ask my father for help. On occasion, to make ends meet, I did carpentry work or took on a project in plywood and plastic laminate.

My furniture provided a source of satisfaction and pride, but I wasn't so attached to the objects I had made as to mind selling them. The customer was as essential to my identity as a furniture maker as a reader is to a writer's identity as a novelist. Had I been making the furniture and just keeping it for myself, I would have lacked the validation and connection that sending my creations out into the world provided.

I think of the furniture I made in New York as a form of currency. Customers were not just buying desks and coffee tables, which they could have found more readily at furniture stores. Customers were buying desks and tables that had been designed and built by a single individual who did so with passion and integrity. This story was conveyed, in part, by the experience of purchasing furniture directly from its maker. But it was also conveyed by the aesthetic qualities of the furniture itself, with its exposed dovetailing, hand-rubbed oil finish, lovely grain selection, and so on. I was engaged in furniture making as a creative process, the practice of which would help me to forge a good life. The furniture I made was the currency that represented the process, as surely as the paper money of my childhood was backed by the gold in Fort Knox.

If I Only Had a Year

New York was a wonderful adventure and the first place where I fully inhabited my identity as a furniture maker, but it was also highly stressful. I was carrying rents on both my apartment and my workshop and the constant financial struggle made me wistful for the college days, just six years earlier, when I had guiltlessly enjoyed the support of my parents.

During my second spring in New York I experienced several months of severe night sweats, loss of appetite, and extreme fatigue, all of which I attributed to some sort of seasonal depression. Finally,

I took my temperature and found I was running an intermittent fever. At that point I went to a doctor and was hospitalized for tests. By the time I received a diagnosis of Hodgkin's disease, which is a cancer of the lymphatic system, I was too weak to stand at the bathroom sink and shave. Further tests determined that I had stage IIIB Hodgkin's, which translated into a 55 percent chance of surviving for five years, with chemotherapy.

My reaction on being told that I had cancer was not what I might have expected. I was relieved to finally know what I had to deal with and calm at the possibility of fading away. It seemed to me I had already lived a full life, like a well-plotted novel that reaches a satisfying conclusion. I had known deep friendship, true love, loss, and sorrow. I had felt at one with nature and at home in the city. And, critically, I had discovered both a creative capacity within myself and the inner discipline to put it to work. I had become a whole person.

At the time, chemotherapy for Hodgkin's disease was a recent medical breakthrough and still subject to experimental research. The most knowledgeable practitioners were at the National Institutes of Health in Bethesda, Maryland, where I was accepted into a study designed to test two alternative chemotherapy regimens against each other. I will leave out the grim details. Effective palliatives had yet to be invented and the rigors of chemotherapy were enough to make one consider taking one's chances without it. Some people I met along the way did just that, and they are no longer here.

I began six months of outpatient chemotherapy in July of 1979 on a schedule of two weeks on and two weeks off. During the on weeks I stayed with Aunt Mickey and Uncle Ed. Ed was a research scientist at NIH, which is how I found out about the Hodgkin's study in the first place. Later he was to become scientific director of the National Heart Institute and a Fellow of the National Academy of Sciences.

During the off weeks I did my best to retain a sense of normalcy. I had always thought of people with cancer as pariahs, victims who had passed through a doorway to a separate existence. Now, riding a bus into Manhattan after my first round of chemotherapy, I looked at the cross-section of humanity seated with me and realized that any one of them could be going through what I was, or worse. There was no way to tell by looking, just as anyone on that bus looking at me would have assumed that I was healthy and carefree. I understood then that there was no wall between sickness and health. Health was a continuum, and I was still among the living.

In retrospect, I attribute much of my acceptance at death's approach to how exhausted I was. Death seemed an easy transition. My attachment to life began to recover following that first terrible two-week ordeal of chemotherapy, as the fevers and sweats abated and my red blood count started to climb.

Coincidentally, before I was hospitalized I had arranged to sublet my storefront and apartment to friends for the summer. It had been my plan to buy a used car and drive cross-country, visiting music stores to promote a folding music stand I had designed. Now I was scheduled for at least six months of chemotherapy, maybe eight if things didn't go well. The cross-country trip was out. Freed from ordinary responsibilities, I squarely faced the question: What do I want to do with whatever time I might have left?

You have to be careful what you wish for. There I was, back under the shelter of my parents' wings. Given their financial support, I could imagine plenty of options for whatever active time I might have left if chemotherapy failed. I pictured living on a sunlit Greek island, traveling through Europe, or taking a long sailing voyage. I thought about throwing myself into political action or social service. But really, the answer was crystal clear. What I wanted, in every fiber of my being, was the privilege of bringing just one more piece of beautiful furniture into the world. It would be more than a privilege, really. Like a magician or a god, I had found a way to transmute thought into matter.

CHAPTER 5

Heart, Head, and Hand

WHEN THE HARSH LIGHT of cancer threw my priorities into sharp relief, it was clear that furniture making had become my vocation in both the practical and spiritual senses of the word – not just a trade, but also a calling. Through it, I was constructing an identity and a life that, given the chance, I was eager to explore.

What was it that made this craft so compelling? Over the ensuing years I have come to see that some of its rewards may be discovered through the practice of any creative art, while others are deeply rooted in the nature of craft itself – in its singular and pervasive materiality. Unlike writers, composers, and dancers, whose media are words, sound, and bodily movement, a craftsman fashions tangible matter – traditionally wood, clay, metal, glass, or fiber; today almost anything – into enduring objects. Sculpture and painting are the arts most similar to craft in this regard, and certainly there are gray areas where one shades into the other. But the contemporary sculptor or painter is participating in a conversation that often regards material and skill with suspicion, tolerating them as necessary means to conceptual ends. The contemporary craftsman, in contrast, celebrates material and skill and considers them sources of meaning within the work.

Over the next two chapters I would like to consider the nature and rewards of creative practice, as exemplified through craft, in two distinct contexts. The first is the experience of the person who *creates* a craft object. The second is the experience of a person who *encounters* a craft object. For lack of a better word, I call this second person the object's respondent. In this chapter, I will suggest that, by virtue of its materiality, the making of craft calls forth a symphony of human capacities that are intrinsically fulfilling to the craftsman. In the next, I will suggest that a craft object can be a potent source of meaning and identity for both maker *and* respondent, because it is the essential nature of humanity to engage in what the title of one book on my shelf calls *Thinking with Things*.[10]

During the many years I cut every mortise by hand, I would mark out the shoulders with a knife and square, then scribe the cheeks with a mortise gauge. In both cases I was incising lines onto wood, but there was logic to using different tools. A knife tip severs wood fibers cleanly across the grain, but tends to lodge between fibers and wander when pulled with the grain. The pins of a gauge do pretty much the opposite. They tear wood fibers crudely across the grain, but leave precise tracks with the grain. Using each tool in the correct orientation is essential. The marks they leave behind must precisely locate the cutting edge of a chisel when it comes time to chop the finished edges of the shoulders and pare the cheeks, after the bulk of the waste has been drilled out.

Understanding the mechanics of marking tools was only a tiny part of cutting a mortise. To use chisels well, I had to learn to sharpen them properly, a discipline worthy of graduate study in and of itself. To engineer a joint that was sufficiently strong and durable, I had to understand wood strength, wood movement, grain direction, and properties of adhesives. To perform the work accurately and efficiently, I had to exercise a degree of physical coordination that came only with constant practice. To achieve consistent quality in terms of fit and finish, I had to marshal qualities of character such as focus, patience, and perseverance. All that just for mortises, which are but the hundredth part of making a piece of furniture!

When I was a novice, every step in woodworking required conscious deliberation. Even something as simple as making the hard edges of a table top friendly to the touch meant that I had to think about the extent to which I wanted to "break" them, whether I should chamfer or round them, and a host of other questions. Should I use a file, a rasp, sandpaper, a block plane, a router, or some combination of the above? Was the plane sharp enough? How wide should the plane's throat be open? What grit of sandpaper should I start with? Should I sand freehand or with a sanding block? Should the block have a hard face or a soft face? As you might imagine, with so many decisions, work progressed haltingly. But by the time I had been at it for ten years, these decisions had become second nature. I had worked through the variables to arrive at consistent choices, habits of work that suited my temperament and aesthetic. My hands had learned the difference between overpowering a saw, chisel, or gauge and listening to the tool. If I was making a set of chairs, the work of any particular day might have included drafting, tuning up machinery, milling rough boards into accurately sized components, building forms and laminating curves, making jigs and fixtures, cutting joinery, shaping, scraping, sanding, assembly, and/or finishing. Whatever it was, for long periods of time my ordinary consciousness was subsumed in a dance of making where not a motion was wasted. This is not to say I wasn't thinking – just that I had become far more adept at making decisions. Mind, hand, and body were reading from the same page; they worked together seamlessly.

My father had opined that woodworking would leave me intellectually unfulfilled. But I found that even so simple an operation as cutting a mortise harmonizes intellect, manual skill, and character in a way that underscores the artificiality of the Cartesian divide between mind and body. When you add the creative component of design, craft becomes a fully integrated application of one's capacities. Describing this unity, the influential English ceramicist Bernard Leach wrote: "A potter is one of the few people left who uses his natural faculties of heart, head and hand in balance – the whole man."[11]

Leach's phrasing implies a fall from an imagined state of grace, revealing his roots in the British Arts and Crafts Movement. But without romanticizing preindustrial society, it is still possible to say that craft offers a holistic experience many contemporary Americans find lacking in their occupations and personal lives. I hear this often from my students, particularly those who work in corporate environments where individual effort is engulfed in a collective enterprise, where results are often as ephemeral as numbers on a computer screen, and where the work of the mind is generally segregated from the work of the hand.

One of my great pleasures is sailing Penobscot Bay. Many years ago, when I was shopping for a boat, one of my major criteria was that she steer with a tiller rather than a wheel. Grasping a tiller transmits the action of the rudder directly to the hand, whereas a wheel is more indirect, being connected to the rudder via pulleys. Like most sloops, the one I found has a weather helm under sail, which means she will turn her bow into the wind when left to her own devices. Grasping the tiller, my hand knows just how much countering force to exert on the rudder to keep her on course at any given moment. This, in turn, tells me (in concert with my other senses) how well the mainsail and jib are balanced, how strong the wind is, and how close to the wind I am sailing. The boat becomes a live thing in my hand, but more than that, it is as if my senses extend throughout the boat

– until water, wind, and sky are all there is. Skilled woodworking is like that. My consciousness comes to inhabit the tip of the knife and the tooth of the saw, so that I am not only in the world, but somehow of the world.

Through personal experience, acquaintance with hundreds of other craftspeople, and interaction with thousands of students, I have witnessed the pleasure and empowerment that skilled craftwork offers. There is a deep centeredness in trusting one's hands, mind, and imagination to work as a single, well-tuned instrument, a centeredness that touches upon the very essence of fulfillment. What better way to inhabit one's selfhood to the maximum than exercising one's innate human capabilities productively and powerfully, like an engine firing smoothly on all pistons?

Autotelism

In *The Craftsman*, Richard Sennett defines craftsmanship as "learning to do something well, for its own sake" and makes a plea for extending this attitude into all areas of human endeavor.[12] In *Creativity*, sociologist Mihaly Csikszentmihalyi makes a similar claim for creativity in general where he says:

> Creative persons differ from one another in a variety of ways, but in one respect they are unanimous. They all love what they do. It is not hope of achieving fame or making money that drives them: rather, it is the opportunity to do the work that they enjoy doing.[13]

Both authors are being somewhat idealistic – the desire to do a thing well for its own sake is not universal among craftspeople, nor are all creative people immune to the lures of wealth and fame – but their essential observation rings true. There is great satisfaction to be found in work that engages one as an end in itself.

Csikszentmihalyi theorizes that the intrinsic pleasure of creative work derives from a mental phenomenon he calls *flow*, which is the same experience that I described earlier as a "dance of making." He identifies nine main elements that characterize it:

1. There are clear goals every step of the way.
2. There is immediate feedback to one's actions.
3. There is a balance between challenges and skills.
4. Action and awareness are merged.
5. Distractions are excluded from consciousness.
6. There is no worry of failure.
7. Self-consciousness disappears.
8. The sense of time becomes distorted.
9. The activity is autotelic, i.e., it becomes an end in itself.[14]

I have only two minor quibbles with this list. The first is that, in my experience, the possibility of failure is always present in the workshop. Success and failure are magnetic poles to which I orient my compass at every moment to determine whether or not to take (or persist in) a given course of action. The second is that Csikszentmihalyi's description of flow mixes generative conditions, the first three elements, with descriptive conditions, the final six. One might properly say, *If* there are clear goals every step of the way, immediate feedback, and balance between challenges and skills, *then* action and awareness may merge, distractions may be excluded from consciousness, and so forth.

But what particularly interests me is the precise correspondence between Csikszentmihalyi's ninth element, autotelism, and Sennett's characterization of craftsmanship as doing work well for its own sake. Csikszentmihalyi makes it clear that autotelism can be experienced in many fields of endeavor, and certainly in all creative arts. So to the extent that Sennett's specific choice of a craftsman as his poster child – as opposed to, say, a research scientist or a poet – was warranted, I suggest it is because craft's pronounced materiality so effectively offers the clear goals and immediate feedback that are

Csikszentmihalyi's first and second generative conditions for loving
what you do.

Grounding the Narrative

This brings us to another way of describing the elephant, which is
that craft is especially fulfilling because its materiality anchors the
craftsman's understanding – the stories, ideas, and beliefs through
which he structures his identity, organizes experience, and makes
decisions – in reality. The maker sees the immediate effect of every
step he takes along the way. When his work is concluded, the fruit of
his labor stands there, unambiguously.

Every material has distinctive physical properties, which gov-
ern the ways it can be worked. Wood, for example, can be shaped
by additive and subtractive processes, and even bent to a limited
degree, but it cannot be cast like metal, formed like clay, or knotted
like fiber. Among species of wood there are significant variations
in color, grain, porosity, density, pliability, stability, strength, rot
resistance, and other working qualities. Within smaller parameters,
the same factors vary among boards of the same species, and even
within a single board.

To work his medium successfully, the craftsman adapts to its
character and quirks, even as he subjects it to his will. Over time he
learns to read his material through its response to hand and tool.
The sibilance of a plane tracks the thickness of the shaving, the set
of the blade, the flatness of the board, and the direction of the grain.
Interpreting what he hears, feels, and sees, the craftsman does not
have the luxury of ambiguity. Soon enough, his beliefs are subject
to the test of the real. Either the chisel is sharp enough to pare wood
effectively or it isn't. Joints are tight or have gaps. Surface grain is
smooth or torn. The sturdiness of a table and the comfort of a chair
are immediately apparent to any observer. Craft is a process of

continuous feedback in which the craftsman's working suppositions are subject to constant fact-checking by the real world.

In the workshop, wishing just won't make it so. The craftsman is forced to come to terms with the physical properties of materials, the mechanical properties of tools, and the real capacity and limits of his own dexterity, discipline, and imagination. In this way, craft's materiality imposes cooperation on the sometimes discordant factions of the mind. By necessity it reconciles the desire to interpret the world in ways that are emotionally gratifying with the countervailing need for accurate information to facilitate effective decision making. Thus the holistic quality of craft lies not only in engaging the whole person, but also in harmonizing his understanding of himself in the world. Matthew Crawford expresses this well in *Shop Class as Soulcraft* where he writes:

> The satisfactions of manifesting oneself concretely in the world through manual competence have been known to make a man quiet and easy. They seem to relieve him of the felt need to offer chattering *interpretations* of himself to vindicate his worth. He can simply point: the building stands, the car now runs, the lights are on. Boasting is what a boy does, who has no real effect in the world. But craftsmanship must reckon with the infallible judgment of reality, where one's failures or shortcomings cannot be interpreted away.[15]

CHAPTER 6

Thinking with Things

AT THE START of the previous chapter I claimed that the craftsman celebrates material and skill as sources of meaning in the work. This is apparent even in a distinctly functional piece, such as the desk at which I write (plate 2). I designed this desk when I was twenty-eight years old and had been in remission from cancer for less than a year. At the time, my stated goal was to create furniture that manifested simplicity, integrity, and grace. As I have come to understand it since, however, my underlying brief was actually to arrive at a vision of how life could and should be lived.

There were three critical aspects to this effort: discovery, embodiment, and communication. They seem to define the essential structure of all forms of creative practice. Discovery is the process of coming up with new ideas and implementing them, decision by decision. Embodiment is the way in which the constructed desk cast my decisions in concrete – became what the painter Chuck Close has referred to as the frozen detritus of the artist's experience.[16] Communication is what happens when the desk registers on the consciousness of a respondent.

DISCOVERY

Design was discovery, from the first tentative sketch to the hundreds of aesthetic choices that I made during the desk's construction, such as deciding how far the top should overhang the sides and what the

arc of the stretcher should be. What was I discovering? I was thinking my way visually – thinking with materials and tools, rather than
with words – toward an object that would reveal the nature of a good
life. Furniture, after all, is more than an object of contemplation; it is
a prescription for the life to be lived around it. All the world may be a
stage, but for the most part it comes preset with inherited props. The
furnishings among which we play out our lives – a Sheraton dining
chair, a print of Monet's *Water Lilies at Giverny*, a Hummel figurine,
a Kenmore refrigerator – express the time-bound perspectives of
the people who made them, just as they may reflect the prejudices,
passions, and predilections of the people who own them. They are
cues that convey meaning, shape our identities, and provide us with
a sense of continuity. Inescapably, we are beings for whom objects
have spiritual weight.

A single piece of furniture articulates a point of view about life on
many levels. I'll identify three. First, as an aesthetic whole, it positions
itself within a thick cultural narrative of style and meaning. Thus this
particular desk – with its streamlined traditional form, absence of
hardware, natural wood, overt functionality, and exposed, hand-cut
dovetails – speaks of both Shaker and modernist design precepts.
It orients the contemporaneous respondent, consciously or not, to
the Shaker view that domestic life and work should be lived as sacra-
ments. At the same time, it connects him to the ethos of design icons
such as Charles and Ray Eames, Eero Saarinen, Alvar Aalto, and
Marcel Breuer, who embraced modernity and whose work spoke to
new horizons of human potential.

Second, as an aggregation of physical details, this desk conveys
a hundred distinct impressions, all of which evoke meaning. The
perfection of a dovetail, the beauty of the wood, the clarity and
depth of the finish, the silky touch, the care taken with the back of a
drawer, the continuous grain of the front apron as it flows through

the drawer faces: each transports its silent freight of information. Each implies, by what it is and what it is not, the orientation of the craftsman toward work, as well as toward workmanship, nature, beauty, tradition, and human character. Together, the details reveal an extraordinary investment of time, care, and skill in a functional object intended for the home. They read as an argument for the value and dignity of daily domestic life.

Third, as a manifestation of craftsmanship, the desk is at odds with our society's rampant consumerism. It speaks of durability at a time when most goods are disposable. It speaks of integrity of process in a culture where surface impressions are often all that matter. Consumerism promises spiritual and emotional fulfillment through acquisition. Buy the right car, designer purse, or trendy footwear and you'll find happiness. But the physical details of the desk speak to a more ancient materialism, deep in the human psyche. This is the belief that objects have mana: that the miraculous power to provide spiritual sustenance resides in the object itself, not in the achievement of ownership. We enshrine the original manuscript of the Declaration of Independence because it has mana; we revere hallowed paintings in museums because they have mana; we make pilgrimages to the Shroud of Turin because it has mana.

In short, in making a straightforward desk I utilized a language of materiality that was simultaneously visual, tactile, stylistic, spiritual, functional, and political to *design* my way to a vision of a good life. At the same time, by transforming lumber into a desk in order to earn my livelihood, I was constructing an actual life. With myself as the guinea pig, I was experimenting with the material work of craft to discover how a good life might be lived minute to minute, day to day, month to month, in and out of the workshop. From the first inkling of its design to the last buffing of its tung oil finish, the making of the desk was a multilayered process of thinking with things.

EMBODIMENT

Having already suggested a variety of ways in which craft can be employed to discover, embody, and communicate a point of view about how life should be lived, I would like to emphasize the timeless quality of that embodiment. Once an object is made, it becomes a physical fact of the universe, essentially unchanging in the scale of human time. To the human mind, where thoughts spring up unheralded only to vanish just as capriciously, the object becomes a memory device – a tablet on which the maker inscribes a complex of ideas so that he can have recourse to them for further thinking.

One aspect of this is that each completed work becomes a springboard for the genesis of its successors. As a maker I have the luxury of responding to the visual, tactile, and functional qualities of a finished piece over time. I observe the responses of others. I sense what works aesthetically and practically – and what does not. What I learn informs subsequent creative efforts, through which I strive for a more compelling and accurate vision.

The pleasure I experience when the coffee table in our living room catches my eye is a good example of the way that an object functions as a thought marker. The table itself is small and simple. I built it two years ago as a private homage to Alan Peters, a British furniture maker of the preceding generation whom I greatly admire (plates 3A and 3B). Alan trained in the 1940s in the workshop of Edward Barnsley, a scion of the Cotswolds Arts and Crafts tradition. When he started, the shop was still not electrified, so the floor was usually ankle-deep in plane shavings. All of the craftsmen smoked, and one of young Alan's responsibilities as an apprentice was to shovel shavings outside whenever a discarded cigarette set them on fire. When "the governor," as the workmen called Barnsley, decided to bring electricity into the workshop, fierce disputes broke out among the workmen about the propriety of hanging a single light bulb. From the time he started his own workshop in the 1960s, Alan worked long and hard to prove that one could still earn a living in the contemporary world by building useful, beautiful furniture with integrity, one piece at a time. He took pride in making furniture that was priced within reach of working people like himself. In the public mind, he eventually became the living avatar of the British Arts and Crafts furniture movement. The queen decorated him with the Order of the British Empire for advancing that tradition into the present with innovative design.

The coffee table that I created consists of only three pieces of wood. A thick slab of air-dried, Maine-grown black walnut bridges two upright legs sawn from a two-inch-thick maple plank. The underside of the top is curved to follow the natural sweep of the growth rings (plate 4). What saves the table from rustic chunkiness is that every visual surface is crisply fluted, except for the polished walnut end grain, which is especially lovely for not having been steamed. (Commercially harvested walnut logs are usually steamed to diffuse into the pale sapwood the minerals that color the dark heartwood. In theory, this lets sapwood pass for heartwood. In fact, the rich, varied hues of the heartwood, which include greens and purples and a whole palette of browns, are muddied to uniform dullness, while the sapwood never darkens sufficiently.)

Simplicity, fluting, and the decorative use of end grain were signature elements of Alan Peters's design vocabulary. Using them, the table captures the essence of what I so admire about his work and the way he went about it. British furniture makers of my generation have come to dinner, looked at the table, and exclaimed, "Oh, Alan Peters!" Yet I am sure that my inward smile in the early morning, when I walk through the living room en route to this study, is not for Alan Peters. I rarely think of him when responding to the table. My heartbeat of pleasure is unmediated by conscious thought or association. In small part, it is a glow of satisfaction at having brought so pleasing an object into being. Mostly, though, it is the visual aesthetic of the table that affects me.

I cannot dissect the mechanics of visual pleasure: how formal qualities such as proportion, color, and texture combine with cultural associations to make an object luminous. I can, however, identify a few visually transmitted qualities that make this particular coffee table pleasing to me, and perhaps to others, whether or not they have heard of Alan Peters. One is the unexpectedness of the corrugated table top. Another is the succession of discoveries that pulls you across the room: at a distance the overall form is attractive; as you draw near the play of light upon fluting commands your eye; up close, the natural beauty of the wood reveals itself.

A third aspect of the table's appeal is the tension between the elemental character of its material and structure on the one hand, and the refinement of its surfaces on the other. The blocky legs and half-round top bring to mind heavy timbers and rudimentary construction, while the precise half-round channeling of the flutes conveys the refinement of classic high-style furniture. Wood grain and color pipe a feral, ancient tune beneath a formal cadence of fluting (somewhat like the wail of coyote in the marsh below our house, to which I awaken, safe and warm, on a wintry Maine night). What makes these contrasts appealing is more than a visual harmony of form and color; it is the ideas they express in a language that bypasses words.

Earlier I said that furniture describes the life to be lived around it. This table suggests a complementary balance between rawness and cultivation, nature and civilization. The vision it expresses is my own, but I have voiced it in a vocabulary that Alan Peters explored throughout a lifetime of design and construction. The table is not just a static record of the moment of its making. It is a thought marker for a complex, evolving ideal, both personal and societal.

COMMUNICATION

In many ways, the coffee table in my living room and the desk at which I sit are like the book that you are reading. Each came into being through a creative process in which I explored ideas about life. When I am making furniture, I think with things; when I am writing, I think with words. Both methodologies are powerful tools.

Likewise, both coffee table and manuscript embody questions I asked and the answers at which I arrived during their creation. Being permanent and accessible in a way that thought isn't, they serve as landmarks for my further exploration. Yet I am not the only possible respondent and reader, nor was I intended to be. My hope from the start has been to participate in a larger conversation by creating something worth sharing. And even if I were the most reclusive of furniture makers or most private of diarists, I would still be watching my furniture take shape through the eye of a hypothetical user, just as I listen to my prose through the ear of a theoretical reader. Such is human nature. We are socially embraided to such an extent that the architecture of our thoughts is a communal construction. Anything I create becomes a doorway through which others can access my ideas and concerns, if they care to.

Admittedly, there is plenty of room for ambiguity, error, and misconstruction when someone peers through that door. As a general rule, the more closely a respondent shares a maker's cultural orientation, the more accurate his reading of an object or text will be. But the maker has limited control over the respondent's takeaway. In part, this is because what get embedded in the work are not only questions and ideas of which the maker is conscious, but also attitudes and hypotheses of which he remains unaware. In part, it is because a person's worldview uniquely informs what he notices and how he interprets it. As a result, an important measure of any maker's success is the transparency of his creation. How accurately and comprehensively does the object convey his interests and intuitions?

Although both furniture and books carry ideas, there are significant differences between them, such as how they sequence information. Reading text is a linear progression where one idea follows another like the news crawl at the bottom of a television screen. On the positive side, this gives a writer significant control of the step-by-step process through which a reader accesses ideas. On the downside, only one thought can be presented at a time. The remainder of the author's composition is either receding into the netherworld of memory or invisibly waiting in the wings for its moment on stage. In contrast, a craft object is a collage in which many pieces and levels of information are read in relationship to each other in the present. When I look at a piece of furniture from across a room, I see form, style, scale, context, and intended use. As I approach it, I distinguish material, joinery, and proportions. When I get close enough to touch it, I take in details such as hardware, textures, finish, edge treatments, wood grain, quality, and comfort. A craftsman cannot control a respondent's path through this information as tightly as an author, but the craftsman has the advantage of making complex structures of information simultaneously apparent. His picture is worth the proverbial thousand words.

While I have used the examples of a desk and a table, I might have referred with equal success to genres of craft that are more sculptural in intent, or to works of art from other fields. Whether a maker chooses to employ function, nonfunction, or dysfunction to make his point, or practices an art to which the question of function is irrelevant, he goes through a similar process of thinking with things (such as material, sound, movement, and language) to discover, embody, and communicate a vision of what matters.

The Meaning of Objects

The meaning that a respondent detects in a work of art may or may not have anything to do with the information that has been coded into it by the maker. Once it enters the world, an object gathers history and associations on its own. The flag draping a fallen soldier's casket has far greater significance for the mourner who takes it home than would any identical flag.

In addition, the meanings that respondents project onto an object often have nothing whatsoever to do with the maker's intentions. When European and American art museums began collecting "African art" in the early twentieth century, curators enshrined ceremonial and functional African objects for aesthetic visual qualities that happened to resonate with contemporary styles in Western art. They were often clueless about the objects' actual meanings and functions.

The distinction between the information an object carries and the meaning it has is critical. Information is intrinsic and permanent. It resides in the object's physical characteristics, which are an unchanging record of thousands of decisions made by its maker during its creation. Meaning, on the other hand, is extrinsic and subjective. It resides in the minds of respondents, and will differ among them, just as two readers may arrive at widely divergent interpretations of the same text.

To say that an object has *meaning* (or is *meaningful*) is to use the word differently than when one talks about the meaning of life. One could say that a person's life has meaning, for him, to the extent that he feels his own thoughts and actions make a moral difference in a larger sphere. But when we say an object has meaning, we are not measuring its moral import. Instead, we are measuring its emotional importance to a respondent.

Often, the most meaningful objects are the most mundane. A woman whose house was destroyed by Hurricane Katrina said that what she most regretted losing were family snapshots from her childhood. A person who has time to retrieve only one object from a burning house is more likely to stumble out of the smoke clutching a parent's wedding ring or a family Bible passed down through generations than his most expensive piece of electronic equipment. How do humble heirlooms and mementos attain such overriding emotional significance? They become, I would suggest, talismans that independently confirm their owners' central narratives of personal identity.

After all, to maintain the stories that constitute one's understanding of oneself in the world is a constant struggle, not just because memory is frail, but because the world around us swarms with contrary facts and alternative viewpoints. We need all the help we can get, especially when it comes to narratives that are ours alone or that we share with only a few other people. A giant flat-screen television may have meaning, but the story it conveys is less critical to its owner's self-image than that told by a family heirloom, and, being shared among far more people, considerably less fragile.

The Oriental rug on my study floor is an example of the sturdy meaning an ordinary household object might have. The carpet confirms aspects of my identity such as taste, class, and relative affluence. But any one of ten thousand Oriental rugs could do the same, which is one reason why this carpet is not nearly so meaningful to me as a framed embroidery of the Lord's Prayer that hangs in the hallway upstairs, hand-stitched by a grandmother I never knew. There is only one such sampler in the world, and the family history it confirms is highly perishable, being of direct interest to only six living people.

Some of the most common ways in which a craft object attains meaning for a respondent are through information coded into the object by the maker; through the experience of discovering or acquiring the object; through a personal connection with the maker; and through provenance or projection. The object may acquire meaning at first contact – it may, as one passionate crafts curator recently said to me, "touch your heart" – or it may accrue meaning over years of use. However it happens, objects ultimately possess meaning to the extent that they affect or confirm the stories through which a respondent constructs his identity and orders his world. The more central those narratives are, the more meaning the object has.

The Object as Emissary

In Nantucket, Maryland, and New York I was forging an adult identity through the process of becoming a craftsman. In great part, that transformation took place through the hands-on work of furniture making, which shaped my consciousness daily. The objects I made had significance for me because they embodied my evolving ideas and beliefs. But at the same time, to truly assume the identity of a craftsman, I needed to inform my social environment so that others would see me that way, too. After all, constructing an identity is not a self-contained project. One's sense of self is a fluctuating assemblage of beliefs and feelings strongly influenced by external circumstances, especially the beliefs of other people. To become a craftsman I had to coax the narratives of others down the trail I was blazing. The things I made were emissaries sent out into the world to negotiate on my behalf. They influenced the beliefs of others regarding my occupation and capabilities.

While the effort to form an identity is flagrantly apparent in the young, it is not limited to youth. We work assiduously at all ages to maintain personal narratives that satisfy us and to see the self-image that we prefer reflected back in the eyes of others. It begins every morning with our choice of clothing, and proceeds from there. For a craftsman, making is a lifelong project of self-construction and self-determination.

In conclusion, it would be difficult to overemphasize the degree to which the materiality of craft in particular, and creative work in general, are effective sources of fulfillment, meaning, and identity for both maker and respondent. We think with materials and objects at least as much as we think with words, perhaps far more. They are conduits through which we construct our selves and our world.

CHAPTER 7

Exercising My Voice

CANCER, at age 27, had been a grim twist of fate, and chemotherapy was a tremendous test of will. Worst were the long hours when my entire awareness contracted to a flickering red speck of instinct. There was no thought, no sense of "I" in the thing that curled into a ball on a spare bed at Mickey and Ed's between recurrent bouts of vomiting and dry heaves. I wouldn't let anyone near me. I was, literally, an animal that had ingested poison and crawled off to die.

Every time I took myself to the hospital for another round of drugs it was like forcing my hand onto a red-hot stove. Just driving to the hospital, parking, and walking in the door was a challenge. The week I started, they were putting a new entryway on the building. Every time I walked into the hospital for the next six months, the chemical odor of fresh-cut plexiglass greeted me. That smell alone was enough to render me nauseated, both then and for years afterwards, no matter where I encountered it.

The good news was that the first round of chemotherapy significantly blasted away the cancer. My hold on life strengthened considerably. Night sweats ceased. The fever abated. My red blood count started to climb back towards normal. In the two weeks after my first round, I went to visit friends in the Hamptons, out near the eastern tip of Long Island. There, spending time at the beach, I briefly touched the carefree feeling of summer I'd known during school vacations. After my third round, at the beginning of September, I moved my shop and belongings from New York City to the village of Wainscott in the Hamptons, where I rented a garage apartment a mile from the beach. I lived upstairs, set up my workshop downstairs, worked as much as I could, and took afternoon walks by the sea.

Friends from the city helped me move out. We arrived on a beautiful late-summer afternoon and went to the beach for a few hours before unloading the van. On the warm sand, swimming with friends in the surf, borrowing a family's canvas raft, I experienced a joy so transcendent that, strange as it sounds, I perceived something I can only describe as a halo of light around my head, such as one sees crowning a saint in a medieval painting. This was not happiness; it was bliss. All my life desires had been pared down to one, which was to be without pain or discomfort, and there on the beach my wish was fulfilled. I wanted for nothing.

What unleashed bliss was the absolute cessation of wanting, which had been so ubiquitous that it had to disappear entirely before I could see it. Prior to cancer, my existence had been scored to a steady bass line of long-term desires and a staccato beat of immediate ones – desires as transient as winning a game of chess, as practical as meeting a deadline in the workshop, as compelling as finding love, as materialistic as wanting a new car, as pedestrian as looking for comfortable shoes. I wanted respect, I wanted to be attractive, I wanted people to like me. I had been a want-generating machine. Without the distraction of wanting, I became alive to the moment, and the moment was incomparable. The bliss I experienced on the beach was what I imagine people strive for who hope to be "one with the universe."

So it was that, during the interludes between rounds of chemotherapy, I experienced some of the most serene, joyous times of my life. Cancer had spun the kaleidoscope and the bits and pieces were rearranging themselves in new patterns.

Finding My Voice

In January of 1980, having completed six months of chemotherapy, I was at home in Wainscott waiting for the phone to ring. I still remember the apprehension with which I picked up the receiver. The person on the other end of the line was a doctor from NIH with the results of my restaging – the surgery and tests I had recently undergone to determine whether I would need two additional months of chemotherapy. The news was good. I was in remission. I hung up and, for the first time in all those long months, I cried. Actually, I sobbed uncontrollably, overwhelmed with gratitude and relief.

I was alone when I received the call, but not alone in the world. I had my parents, I had good friends, and I had a lovely girlfriend – an aspiring actress whom I had met on the Wainscott beach. During the four years since my relationship with Gail had ended I had dated a number of women, but I had remained too preoccupied with the loss of my first love to form any real attachments. My stubborn heart mourned, no matter how much my head and nether parts told it to move on. Now cancer had swept through my life like a tsunami, destroying familiar landmarks and leaving behind a cleansed terrain in which the failure of my first love was easier to accept, and new love became possible.

Even so, I lived a relatively solitary life in Wainscott, and furniture making was my focus. I had been in the process of marketing the adjustable wooden music stand when I fell ill, and while I was enduring chemotherapy it received pre-Christmas publicity in *Esquire*, *The New Yorker*, *House & Garden*, and *New York Magazine*, as well as a listing in the Horchow Collection mail-order catalog. Scores of people ordered them as Christmas presents. Unfortunately, as December approached, it became clear that the commercial shop I had hired to produce the stands in my absence wasn't going to complete them on time. The wooden parts were done, but the time-consuming hardware installation wasn't. The upshot was that two kindly friends came out to Wainscott for an intense week of assembly and packing, and we had a hundred stands ready just in time for Christmas shipping.

Aside from the music stands, I was marketing my work primarily through craft shows. In 1978, I had been accepted to the American Craft Council's Northeast Craft Fair, the WBAI Holiday Craft Fair in New York City, the Berkshire Crafts Fair, and the Philadelphia Museum of Art Craft Show. Mostly I sold one-of-a-kind pieces that I made speculatively, and took orders for variations on the same. Occasionally, someone commissioned a new design. But after years of being inspired by various historical styles – Shaker, Early American, Arts and Crafts, Art Nouveau, Scandinavian, Chinese – I was becoming aware that my work needed a distinctive, compelling look. A person entering a gallery or seeing a photograph ought to be able to say to himself, "That must be a Korn." Otherwise, I didn't see how I was going to sell enough work, and at high enough prices, to provide a sustainable living.

From day one of making furniture on Nantucket, I had been sketching furniture designs that would advance my skills and please me visually. Now I began sketching to find an aesthetic of my own. A sculptor I met in the Hamptons gave me some valuable advice. He suggested that I consider the appearance of the negative spaces between and around the solid components of a piece of furniture. Had I been formally educated in art or design, I would have learned this as a freshman. In any case, it was good advice because shortly thereafter a chair appeared under the tip of my pencil that was different than anything I'd designed before (plate 5). It was spare, functional, attractive, and, most importantly, it didn't reference any historical style. It was mine alone and it pleased me.

Not long after, the same thing happened a second time, only better. An elegant, purposeful dictionary stand appeared in my

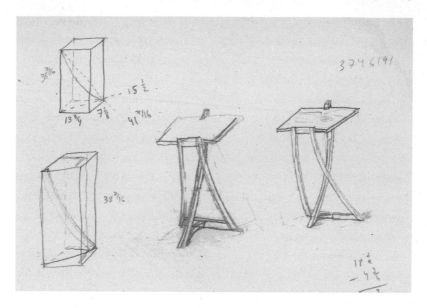

The dictionary stand (center and right) as it first appeared in
the author's sketchbook.

sketchbook, with graceful curves and compound angles that would
push my joinery skills hard (plate 6). It would be juried into exhibitions,
win some modest awards, and sell reasonably well. I had found my
voice. It was time to use it.

Community

In the spring of 1981, I had my first solo show. It took place at the
Gross McCleaf Gallery in Philadelphia, and the opening was
an unexpected embrace, a homecoming. People attended whom
I hadn't seen since high school, twelve years previously – my favorite history teacher, Mrs. Reifsnyder, my Aunt Betty, friends of my
parents, old schoolmates – people I had known since childhood who
were genuinely delighted to see what I'd done. This was a feeling

of belonging that had been missing in Nantucket, Frederick, New York, and Wainscott, only I hadn't recognized its absence. I had fled the community in which I grew up in order to forge my own identity. Now I discovered that my hometown gave context to my journey in a way no other place could.

The work at Gross McCleaf included the side chair and dictionary stand through which I had recently found my voice, plus earlier pieces such as an English brown oak wall cabinet inspired by the ski-jump profile of a traditional Norwegian roof, a walnut stool inspired by Chinese furniture, and an Art Nouveau–inspired folding screen in cherry, stretched with raw silk on which a friend, Lynn Goodpasture, had painted irises.

It was a buoyant time. Not only was I was making the transition from craft shows to art galleries, but a writer I admired, George Trow, had visited my Wainscott workshop for an upcoming Talk of the Town piece in *The New Yorker*. Also, I had been invited to manage the woodshop of a summer arts program in Colorado. Most importantly, my health remained good. I had been in remission for a year and a half, and the longer I stayed in remission, the better my chances of survival became. I measured life differently than before. Where once time had been a seamless highway rippling into the future, now it was a toll road punctuated by checkups at NIH. These had initially been monthly, then quarterly, then semiannual. Eventually they would become annual, which is how I still experience life: yearlong journeys bookended by physical exams every December.

From the start, there was a pattern to those checkups that belied my buoyancy. Weeks or months in advance, I would discover swollen lymph nodes in my neck, or have night sweats, or become tired and lethargic. Try as I might to remain calm, the fear that formed the weak background radiation of my life would rapidly condense to critical mass. Panicked, I would telephone to move the appointment up. And every time it turned out that the lump I felt was some normal body part, or I had been sleeping with too many blankets, or perhaps anxiety had made me tired.

By the time I put my belongings into storage and pointed my van toward Colorado in June of 1981, I was no longer the blissful spirit who had endured six months of chemotherapy. During eighteen months in remission my earthly character had reasserted itself as inexorably as water seeps back into a pumped-out quarry. Once again I was a person who wanted, with my own generous helping of competitiveness, selfishness, and insecurity. But that wanting, that character, was now tempered with the knowledge of my own impermanence. Two things I knew at every moment, deep in my gut: one, that there might not be a next time, and two, that it was only a short walk back through the plexiglass door to the chemo room at NIH.

Anderson Ranch

The furthest west I had ever been was hitchhiking through Texas on my return from Mexico during college. Now I was Colorado-bound, and the Rockies exceeded my expectations. Just beyond the Eisenhower Tunnel, at eleven thousand feet, I pulled onto the shoulder for the experience of throwing a snowball in June. Perhaps it was the lack of oxygen, but the air was intoxicating. The Rockies felt like a world closer to Creation than any I had known.

Anderson Ranch Arts Center, when I finally pulled in, was less than I'd imagined. I had been expecting the Ponderosa, with wild horses galloping in the distance. What I found was a clutter of run-down log cabins and barns on little more than an acre of land, hedged in by the condominiums and golf links of a burgeoning ski resort. I located the director, Jeffrey Moore, in the loft of a barn, brushing bright acrylic paint onto an abstract canvas with the Talking Heads blasting at full volume. Jeffrey was even younger than I was, but his

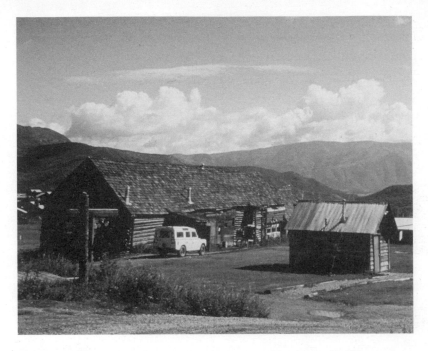

Anderson Ranch Arts Center, circa 1981. Photo by Brad Miller.

height, confidence, and premature baldness gave him a reassuring air of authority.

Anderson Ranch offered summer courses in woodworking, ceramics, painting, weaving, and photography from June through August. The rest of the year it went into hibernation. My job was to maintain the woodshop for the summer, assist the woodworking instructors, and teach a two-week introductory course. Funky as the place was, it attracted an inspiring faculty, including, that summer, Pennsylvania wood turner David Ellsworth and California furniture makers Sam and Slimen Maloof, John Nyquist, and Art Carpenter.

The Ranch was my first exposure to the working methods and creative processes of other craftspeople and artists. At lunch, at parties, at Tex-Mex restaurants, at volleyball, and on mountain hikes, talk flowed continuously, although not necessarily the earnest conversation that one imagines among café artists in 1920s Paris. I learned about being a maker not just from what people communicated purposely, but also from what they did, how they went about doing it, and the attitudes and beliefs that informed even the most casual conversations.

Some things I learned were offered didactically, such as a painter advising me to sketch curves with continuous lines rather than tentative dashes. Some were offered indirectly, such as hearing others employ a language of formal criticism to evaluate work through lenses such as visual weight, symmetry, texture, and intent. But most of what I learned I never even noticed at the time: how artists integrate their self-absorbed passion for making with the necessity of earning a living and the demands of maintaining a relationship. In short, I finally found myself among my own species. The ranch was an ad hoc community of people who were fully engaged with the creative process, people for whom work was a means of exploring identity and constructing original narratives, people for whom life and work were inseparable.

In September, as the aspen leaves yellowed and the snowline crept stealthily down the mountain sides, Anderson Ranch emptied down to the few staff who would stay through the winter. Although I had been offered a year-round, part-time position, I decided to return east. Partly this was because the woodshop at the ranch had neither heat nor insulation. Partly it was because I figured that if I was going to build a successful career as a furniture maker, I was most likely to find a clientele in Philadelphia, where I was represented by a downtown gallery and had a built-in community of support. And partly it was because there was a young woman in Philadelphia who was not responding to treatment for Hodgkin's disease and, more than anything else, I wanted to help reverse the course of her illness.

Philadelphia

In October 1981 I drove from Colorado to Philadelphia, where, after weeks of searching, I found my dream workshop. It was three times as large as any previous space I'd had – 1,200 square feet on the third floor of an old stone mill building in Manayunk, with good natural light and high ceilings. I could overlook the fact that it had little heat and no insulation, that the hundred-year-old windows were falling apart, that it lacked both wiring and light fixtures, and that the only access was a narrow back stairway. If it hadn't been so run-down, I couldn't have afforded the rent. Lumber and machinery had to come up from the parking area through a series of trapdoors in an archway. It was startling, that first day, to watch my table saw rise in the air overhead, pulled by an ancient, electric chain hoist bolted to rafters forty feet above.

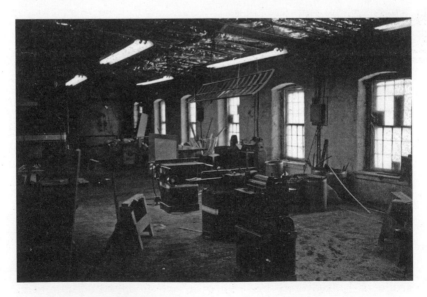

Interior of the Manayunk workshop, 1984.

I paid an electrician to wire and light the shop, and went to work making furniture for clients and galleries. Outside of work, I tried to provide whatever practical and emotional support my friend with cancer would accept. At first I helped with practicalities such as grocery shopping, cooking, and trips to the hospital. But as her health deteriorated, the disparity between our situations seemed to become too much for her. After six months she severed all connection with me; within two years she was dead. Ours was a tangled and difficult relationship, and I attribute much of my own motivation to survivor's guilt – to the unconscious need to justify my own recovered health by saving another. But if cancer had led me into an emotional labyrinth, furniture making was the thread that brought me through. Day by day, I didn't just go to work; to a great extent I *was* my work, and it anchored my life.

During my second year in Philadelphia I was invited to teach furniture design to interior design students at Drexel University, which I did part-time for the next four years. Aside from the summer at Anderson Ranch, this was my first teaching experience, and I became a better furniture maker for it. Communicating about process, design, and aesthetics forced me to translate the tacit knowledge of hand and eye into the conscious realm of language, a realm where it became accessible to rational investigation.

My father tells a story about a woman preparing pot roast for a family gathering. When her husband asks why she cuts the brisket in half and cooks it in two separate pans, she answers, "Because that's how my mother did it." That evening, at dinner, the husband asks his mother-in-law why cooking in two pans makes the brisket better. "Sonny," she says, "I just didn't have a pan big enough to hold a whole roast."

When I began to articulate the furniture making process for my students, I discovered that a lot of my methods and assumptions were like that pot roast – things I did because they worked, without

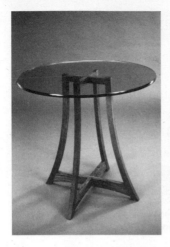 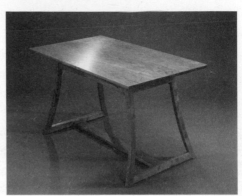

LEFT: English brown oak breakfast table by the author, 32 × 32 × 28½ inches, 1984.
RIGHT: Cherry side table by author, circa 1983.

understanding why. I removed pitch from saw blades with Easy-Off oven cleaner, and only later figured out that hot water from the tap worked just fine. I followed the prescribed steps for putting an edge on a scraper with only variable success, but once I thought through the reason for each step and carefully observed the results, I could sharpen a scraper effectively every time. By way of teaching, I began to engage in woodworking as a science as well as an art.

By 1983, I was showing furniture in galleries in Philadelphia, New York City, Easthampton, Bethesda, Baltimore, and Denver. My aesthetic goal, as I expressed it in an artist's statement, was to make furniture that had the qualities of "simplicity, integrity, and grace." Those were the qualities I discerned in the dictionary stand, and they continued to describe my design exploration for many years thereafter. When possible, I created new pieces that explored the vocabulary of the dictionary stand. But mostly I took orders for things I'd already made, or I designed pieces to customers' criteria. Two of my favorite commissions were a set of cherry dining chairs inspired by the California architects Greene & Greene that I built for a former English teacher from Germantown Friends School, and a cabriole-leg, walnut-burl-veneered desk that I made for a real estate developer who was a client of my father.

Furniture making, at least as I pursued it, was a solitary occupation – eight to twelve hours a day alone in the workshop, with only a radio and my thoughts for company. Rather than being a drawback, though, apartness was central to the enterprise. Even today, most of our professional-track students at the Center for Furniture Craftsmanship dream of having backyard workshops where they can design and build furniture in solitude, interrupted only by collectors pulling up in expensive cars to pay handsomely for their work. Unfortunately, as I try to convey to our students, the desire to work

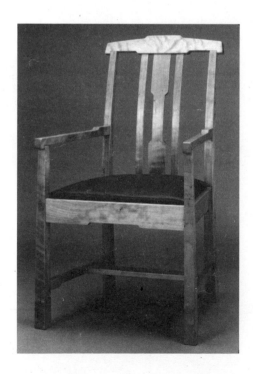

Dining chair designed and made by the author, inspired by the designs of Greene & Greene, cherry, 23 × 22½ × 39 inches, 1984.

alone and apart is self-defeating. There simply isn't enough time in a week to put in sufficient billable hours at the bench and still do all the other work that a successful business requires – maintenance, purchasing, bookkeeping, marketing, customer relations, and so forth. Furthermore, working in isolation doesn't foster the substantial engagement with community it takes to cultivate a local market for custom-made furniture.

The attraction of apartness, I believe, was that it allowed me to construct my own reality independent of intrusive narratives. I had engaged in creative work to create a new story of my self. Working alone, there was little danger of contradiction. But by the time I moved to Philadelphia I was becoming more secure in the identity I had constructed, and my need for isolation was lessening. After a couple of years I took on an informal apprentice. I joined a volleyball league, then initiated and ran a second weekly game in a rented gym at Germantown Friends School. I collaborated with fellow furniture makers to found the Society of Philadelphia Woodworkers and present a juried furniture exhibition at Philadelphia's Port of History Museum. Along the way, I discovered I had a capacity for organization.

Breaks

When I first began making furniture, on Nantucket, I was focused on craftsmanship; design was of secondary importance. Ten years later, in Philadelphia, I had grown confident that I could figure out how to make anything I set my sights on, and some aspects of craftsmanship were starting to feel repetitive, as they inevitably will when you sand six rocking chairs at a time. Meanwhile, design had coyly revealed depths that one could plumb for a lifetime. As a result, I started to look into the possibility of designing freelance for outside manufacturers. It promised all the challenge and excitement of crafting the initial prototype, without the repetition of batch production and the distasteful work of marketing. Especially appealing was the thought of quarterly royalty checks arriving by mail.

When I jumped into furniture making at age twenty-two, I hadn't paused to wonder about its economic potential. From boyhood reading, Quaker education, and Jewish culture I had absorbed the ideas that what mattered in life, respectively, were personal integrity, spiritual fulfillment, and service to community, rather than worldly success. For a long time, therefore, the relative poverty in which I lived as a woodworker seemed of little consequence. That started to change as I entered my thirties. In a world where being an adult meant owning a house and providing for a family, I was out in the cold, looking in at the party. Somehow I was managing to live on a taxable net income of less than $3,000 a year. What seemed to grow year by year was not my income, but a hollow feeling in my chest and a weight on my shoulders.

Amidst this, the ramshackle old mill in which I worked came up for sale. Rather than lose my workshop, I borrowed a small amount of money from my mother, put down a deposit, and signed a purchase agreement that gave me four months to finance and close the deal. With the benefit of free legal counsel from my father, I turned every which way to make the opportunity work. First I tried to turn the mill into condominiums where other craftspeople and artists could purchase affordable studios, until I discovered that banks wouldn't provide mortgages for commercial condominiums. Eventually, I subdivided the complex into three properties and was lucky enough to sell two, keeping the smallest for myself. I walked out of the closing with a check for $20,000 in my pocket and a 5,000-square-foot building free and clear. That was a good feeling. I invested the proceeds, plus a mortgage, in repair and renovation – new windows, new roofs, new heating systems, new plumbing, re-pointed exterior masonry, and so forth. The rent from the other three workshops in the building covered the mortgage, taxes, and insurance, so I ended up with the use of my own workshop for free.

Before signing the purchase contract on the mill I had requested advice from the real estate developer who commissioned the cabriole-leg, walnut desk. He looked at the condition and location of the complex, shook his head in dismay, and pronounced it a white elephant. But I took to the twists and turns of putting together a real estate deal like a duck takes to water. It was eye-opening to discover that I had a capacity for business, that I enjoyed it, and that there was an area where I could earn sizable financial rewards in return for a finite amount of effort.

Not long after, I got another break. The same real estate developer hired me to design and build a reception desk and two sculptures for the lobby of an office building in Florida. It was a $30,000 commission – two to three times what I was grossing in a year. He flew me to Florida to see the building site and we began to explore design opportunities for other real estate projects he had in the pipeline. Finally, after years of knocking, a door had opened onto the vista of a successful career.

The reception desk – an eleven-foot-diameter, forty-two-inch-tall doughnut, divided into three arced segments – was going to be too large to exit my workshop, so I hired a commercial shop to build it to my specifications. For the perimeter I designed a marquetry frieze depicting cranes, both to lighten the desk's considerable visual mass and to acknowledge the wetland habitat that the office building was displacing. I also contracted a friend, Jonathan Scott, to create two life-size bronze sculptures of cranes, for which I built pedestals.

The Dancing Cranes Desk was a major commission, so I invited architects, interior designers, and friends to an unveiling at the gallery of the Moore College of Art. The morning of the opening my father telephoned and asked, "Are you sitting down?" My customer, his client, had just been arrested for embezzling $27 million from

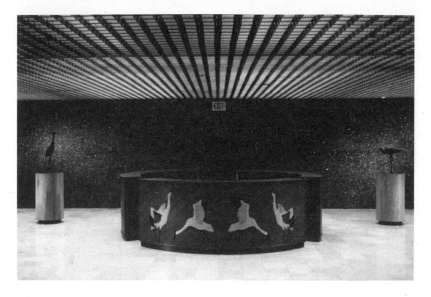

Dancing Cranes Desk, designed by the author, 1984.

the First National Bank of Chicago. I couldn't deliver the desk to Florida, nor was I likely to receive the 50 percent balance due. I did my best to smile as I poured champagne that evening. Months later, the bank would foreclose on the Florida building, and, in an act of generosity, accept delivery of the desk and sculptures and pay the balance due.

My Medici was a jailed sociopath, and my career-transforming commission had hit a dead end. Nevertheless, I had briefly experienced what life was like removed from financial peril, so it was particularly difficult to retreat to a net income of $3,900 in 1985. I felt like the character Joe Btfsplk in *Li'l Abner*, trailed by a personal rain cloud. I even began to resent my customers, because I knew I wasn't charging them enough to make ends meet. In short, my inability to earn a sufficient living was leaching the joy out of furniture making.

The upshot of all this came in September of 1985, when I stopped taking orders for furniture, rented my studio to another woodworker, and gave myself a year to succeed at selling designs to the contract furniture industry. Failing that, I would suck it up and develop real estate. It was time to become an adult.

For the next nine months I spent every day at the drawing board, working in the front room of a dingy shotgun apartment in the suburban town of Ardmore. What I created were pencil renderings of seating collections, which I presented to manufacturers in New York, North Carolina, and Maryland. For income I had a monthly stipend from my father, my salary for teaching at Drexel, and the rent from my workshop. The following June, while I was out in Colorado teaching another two-week course, I signed my first contract – a chair for a manufacturer in Baltimore. I had come in under the wire on my one-year deadline, although signing a contract turned out not to be the same as having my furniture in production and generating sales. When the chair was finally prototyped at the factory, it didn't look nearly as good from the back as it had in the frontal view portrayed in my drawing, so they dropped the project. That would be the last time I submitted chair drawings without first developing a design in three dimensions myself.

Throughout the five years that had elapsed since my first summer there, Anderson Ranch had been offering me a year-round position as woodworking program director. The job came with a small salary, housing, and studio space, and was part-time from September through May, so that I would be able to continue my personal creative work in the off season. By June of 1986 they had winterized the old woodworking barn, so finally I said yes, thinking the job would buy me more time to sell designs. Little did I imagine the extent to which working at the ranch would change the course of my life.

The decision to give up my career as a self-employed furniture maker was neither easy nor happy, although my disappointment was

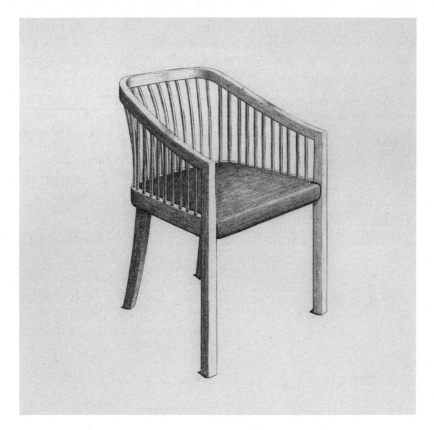

Rendering of the chair design sold to a Baltimore manufacturer.

mitigated by a lifelong predisposition to sprint for the hurdles ahead, rather than look behind in regret at those I have overturned. Glancing back now, though, I see my career as a design process. It began with a brief – to discover a good life – that incorporated assumptions such as "office employment is deadening" and "work should engage both body and mind." My first-draft solution was to become a carpenter, which through trial and error evolved into self-employment as a designer/craftsman making one-of-a-kind, high-end furniture out of wood. The next twelve years were a process of generating, testing, and refining ways of making that career work. My potential for success was limited by flaws inherent in the brief from the start, such as my desire to work alone and apart. Success was also limited by intrinsic properties of the material with which I was working, which was my own self. I was, among other things, not well suited to marketing my work, perhaps because it felt too much like self-promotion, perhaps because it entailed so much rejection.

In design you sometimes have to kill your darlings. This occurs in the happy event that a design takes on a life of its own. One discovery leads to another, until aspects of the brief that had seemed essential at the start become extraneous or limiting and need to be ejected. An impossible brief for a steel stacking chair may lead to a fabulous chair out of molded plastic. When I gave up custom furniture making to try my hand at freelance design, and then took a job at Anderson Ranch, I was not abandoning my life career brief. I was killing some darlings in the light of experience. I had realized during my six years in Philadelphia that financial success mattered, and that I wasn't likely to attain it on the particular path I had chosen. In the years that followed, the main thrust of my career would continue to be the creation of a good life, and the practice of craftsmanship would remain central to it.

CHAPTER 8

The Inward Migration of Truth

WHEN I FIRST hefted a chisel and mallet on Nantucket, the notion of craft that seduced me had strayed some distance from the ideals of the Arts and Crafts Movement. Like any good conversation, craft had embraced new viewpoints and broached new topics. Ruskin and Morris's craftsman was a skilled employee who would produce the designs of others. For my generation, craft was an opportunity to be self-employed, self-expressive, self-sufficient, and self-actualized – the telling word being *self.* We were not particularly self-absorbed for our time and place, however. We were products of an historic shift in the ways an average person understood what it was to be human, where to place the imaginary boundary between personal and social identity, and what the purposes of life were – a shift that deeply affected the practice of all creative arts in the twentieth century. As philosopher Charles Taylor writes:

> … radically different senses of what the good is go along with quite different conceptions of what a human agent is, different notions of the self. To trace the development of our modern visions of the good, which are in some respects unprecedented in human culture, is also to follow the evolution of unprecedented new understandings of agency and selfhood.[17]

For Homer, in ancient Greece, a person had inhabited his full humanity only through action in the public sphere; man's highest aspiration was to achieve recognition in politics and war. For Aristotle, four centuries later, the goal had become a life of detached philosophic contemplation, removed from the dross of domesticity, commerce, politics, and war; a person became fully human only by gazing toward eternal truths. For a medieval Christian, life's goal was to achieve salvation within God's cosmic order. In each period, the self was understood as a component of a larger whole. The source of truth was exterior to the person. By the mid-twentieth century, in contrast, the location of truth had become distinctly internal for many people. The individual stood on his own. The novelist Iris Murdoch characterized this modern, independent self forcefully when she wrote:

> How recognizable, how familiar to us is the man ... who confronted
> even with Christ turns away to consider the judgment of his own con-
> science and to hear the voice of his own reason ... free, independent,
> lonely, powerful, rational, responsible, brave, the hero of so many nov-
> els and books of moral philosophy.[18]

Much as the Arts and Crafts Movement had initiated an important new current in the conversation of object making, the ascendancy of individualism represented a tectonic shift in the conversation of selfhood. The idea of craft that drew me to furniture making in 1974 formed at their confluence.

The Genesis of Studio Craft

Although I began making furniture in a vacuum, it wasn't long before someone sent me a catalog of the 1972 "Woodenworks" exhibition, which had recently been presented at the Smithsonian American Art Museum's Renwick Gallery. It featured work by five leading furniture makers who are today considered founding fathers of contemporary studio furniture. These were Arthur Espenet Carpenter (1920–2006), Wendell Castle (1932–), Wharton Esherick (1887–1970), George Nakashima (1905–1990), and Sam Maloof

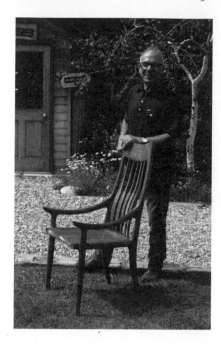

Sam Maloof outside Anderson Ranch
woodshop, circa 1986.

(1916–2009). To a neophyte, they seemed impossibly remote, Promethean elders. Yet the woodworking universe was so thinly populated that within a decade I would assist Carpenter and Maloof in teaching summer workshops, an association in which they assumed decidedly mortal proportions.

That first generation of modern woodworkers was largely self-taught. There were few precedents for what they were attempting, which was to pursue furniture making as a self-expressive, spiritually fulfilling career. Many of them were staunch individualists who would have set out to reinvent the wheel in whatever field caught their fancy.

Art Carpenter was emblematic of that individualism. A man of diminutive physical stature, wry humor, literate intelligence, and genuine modesty, he was the elder whom I found most engaging. Art held an undergraduate degree in economics from Dartmouth and was raised for a career in business. But a four-year stint in the navy convinced him that "being a cog in anyone's machine, other than my own, was not an acceptable consideration."[19] Discharged in 1946, he was casting about for something to do when a bowl by James Prestini caught his eye at the Museum of Modern Art. With no previous woodworking experience, Art drove across the country to San Francisco, bought a lathe, set up shop, and taught himself to turn bowls. One thing led to another. He branched into furniture making and moved to rural Bolinas, California. Eventually, he became a nationally respected craftsman whose legacy includes teaching more than 130 apprentices through the Baulines Craft Guild.

When I first visited Art, in the early 1980s, I found him in a deconstructed dwelling. As he explained it, the San Andreas fault ran through the middle of his property, so he built his house as a cluster of small single-purpose buildings – a kitchen here, a bedroom there, a living room just beyond, and a workshop up the hill – to improve their chances of riding out a seismic cataclysm. This reflected Art's stance as a craftsman, forever perched on the knife-edge of insolvency. He was a close observer who accommodated himself to the nature of things with originality, practicality, and humility, and he abhorred pretense. Decades later, when I paid my final visit, I found the site overgrown, the buildings dilapidated, and Art considerably aged. Pouring wine with a shaky hand that could no long steady a woodworking tool, he explained, with a characteristic wry twinkle, that if his timing was right the entire complex would disintegrate into the earth at the moment of his death.

The origin of the American studio craft movement is generally credited to a small number of post–World War II trail blazers such as Art Carpenter. These include Peter Voulkos (1924–2002) in ceramics, Harvey Littleton (1922–) in glass, and Lenore Tawney (1907–2007) in fiber, among others. People with similar motivations had creatively explored craft media prior to World War II, but Carpenter, Voulkos, et al. were positioned at the historical moment when craft began to benefit from a long demographic surge. It grew slowly through the fifties, a bit faster in the sixties, and then took off in the seventies with the influx of people like myself, participants in the hippie counterculture who were searching for fulfillment through alternative lifestyles.

Unlike proponents of the Arts and Crafts Movement, who had been drawn to a formal ideology, most practitioners of studio craft stumbled into the party. For a long time, there was no concept of "studio craft" as an actual movement. There was only a groundswell: hundreds and then thousands of people made similar life choices, often in relative isolation, each working within mental horizons common to the era. As the pool of craftspeople increased, it provided a fertile environment for the progenitors to influence; it also became a community large enough to embody a shared narrative in which their achievements mattered.

Mihaly Csikszentmihalyi theorizes that creative success requires the interaction of three factors: a creative individual, a field, and a domain. The creative individual generates novel ideas and/or things, but unless he does so within the contexts of a field and a domain, he is just shouting into the wind. A field is a specialized area of knowledge with its own internal language and symbology, such as mathematics or furniture making. A domain is a collection of individuals who decide what belongs in the field and what doesn't, i.e., which mathematical theorems deserve inclusion in the canon of math, which furniture makers are innovating in ways that advance the craft. Csikszentmihalyi writes: "The creative person has internalized a system, has become fluent in the knowledge within a field, so that he has a framework available for editing and evaluating his own ideas, for deciding which ones to go ahead with. He is, in this sense, a product or extension of the domain."[20]

What significantly differentiated the growing field of studio craft from the Arts and Crafts Movement were mutations to the three original strands of craft's intellectual DNA. Over time the romance of the vernacular was balanced by engagement with contemporary trends in art and architecture and the attractions of urban life. The boundary between the fine and applied arts was blurred by makers who explored conceptual and sculptural work from a craft perspective. But most notably, as mentioned above, by the mid-twentieth century the politics of work had transmuted into the politics of "me."

Ruskin and Morris founded their notion of craft on the assumption that the means of production affected the moral development of the worker, and that the objects produced affected the moral development of the consumer. Theirs was an outward orientation. They thought of the individual as a cell within the body politic; their ultimate concern was the health of the social organism. In contrast, practitioners of studio craft such as Carpenter and Voulkos turned inward to focus primarily on their own emotional and spiritual growth. For them, the self was independent and self-sufficient, and the goal of life was to seek fulfillment from within, to maximize their interior capacities for creativity, feeling, experience, and achievement. To the extent that they sought to make the world a better place through craft, they did so by discovering and sharing their personal inner truths.

This inward migration of truth is evident not only in craft, but in all visual arts. Artists are products of their social environments. What they choose to portray, and how they go about it, often betrays what matters most to them. Consciously or not, they invoke the place where truth resides at their cultural moment.

For example, classical Greek sculpture sought to capture an ideal human beauty and perfection that existed outside of time, independent of the individual. Medieval Christian art largely conveyed the contents of the Bible. Renaissance art took on secular themes as individuals turned to secular institutions for identity. Nineteenth-century painters such as J. M. W. Turner and the members of the Hudson River School, who portrayed the raw majesty of the natural environment, were informed by Enlightenment ideals, which found truth in nature, ascribed "natural rights" to the individual, and enshrined the ideal of the noble savage. Late-nineteenth-century impressionists painted the world as it might appear to the eye of an idiosyncratic viewer – they made individual perception, rather than external reality, their true subject.

Tellingly, by the time studio craft emerged fifty years after the rise of impressionism, abstract expressionists were shunning representation of the external altogether. The artist now divined truth entirely from within, as each brushstroke, mark, drip, or splatter registered his internal response to its predecessors on the canvas. The resulting abstract image was neither more nor less than a self-referential record of one person's inner, creative exploration, a portrait of his intuition.[21]

As the location of truth migrated inward, the creative individual took on mythic stature. Art historian Esther Pasztory describes this phenomenon well:

> By the mid-twentieth century the concept of the shaman had been transformed into a metaphor for the artist; the artist is now identified as someone on the edge of madness who can ascend or descend into realms of unconsciousness unavailable to others and bring back gifts for the community in the form of works of art.[22]

This was the zeitgeist that gave birth to the contemporary practice of craft. From the start, the hallmark of studio craft has been the motivation of its practitioners to seek identity, fulfillment, and meaning from within through creative, self-expressive work.

When I chose to become a furniture maker, I was acting on an unexamined worldview that was very much the product of my historical moment. The Industrial Revolution was a fait accompli, and had destroyed the economic foundation for practicing what we now call *craft* as a trade. Prior to the Industrial Revolution, virtually every object had been produced "by hand." Subsequent to it, making things by hand became a potentially subversive act – something one did in opposition to prevailing societal norms.

At the same time that craft was being displaced in the economic order, there was a major shift in how people viewed themselves as individuals. For all of recorded history, beliefs about the nature of humanity and the purposes of life had been in flux, but every major belief system had agreed that a person became fully human only through participation in a larger entity, whether that entity was a tribe, a polity, a divine cosmology, or a social class. By the mid-twentieth century, however, where people had once looked to external sources for validation, truth was now to be found within. With this change, external scaffoldings began to fall away and the task of constructing one's identity became the life project of the individual. The demands of self-definition strongly shaped the nature and practice of craft, in essence converting it to a form of spiritual practice.

Such was the world to which I and other makers of my generation were born. For all the bravado with which we embarked on our voyages of discovery, the poles to which our compasses were oriented had already been determined by the sweep of history.

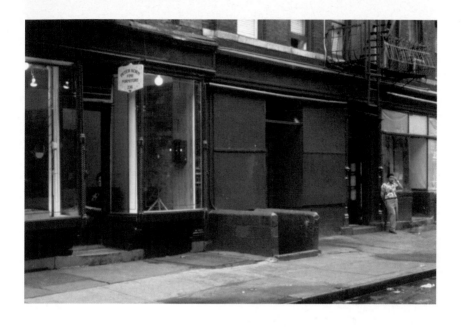

PLATE I. The workshop on Elizabeth Street in New York's Little Italy, 1977.

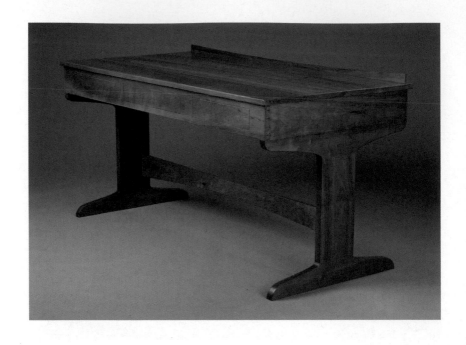

PLATE 2. The author's desk, cherry, 31 × 60 × 31 inches, 1980. Photo by Jim Dugan.

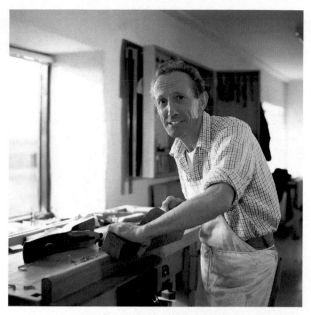

PLATE 3A. Alan Peters at his bench, circa 1999. Photograph by Chris Skarbon, Courtesy of *Furniture and Cabinetmaking*/GMC Publications, UK.

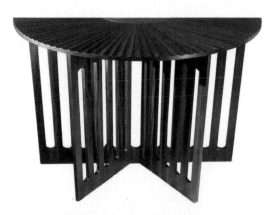

PLATE 3B. Fan Table by Alan Peters, rosewood and satinwood, 48 × 20 × 33 inches, circa 1988.

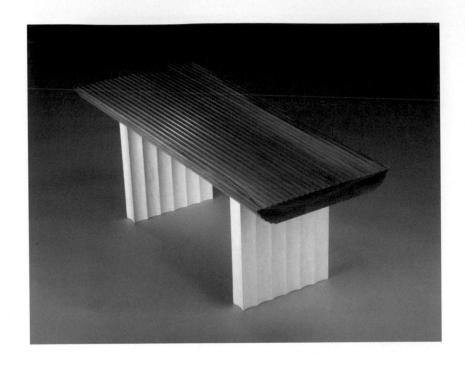

PLATE 4. Fluted Coffee Table by author, walnut and maple, 15 × 38 × 16 inches, 2008.
Photo by Jim Dugan.

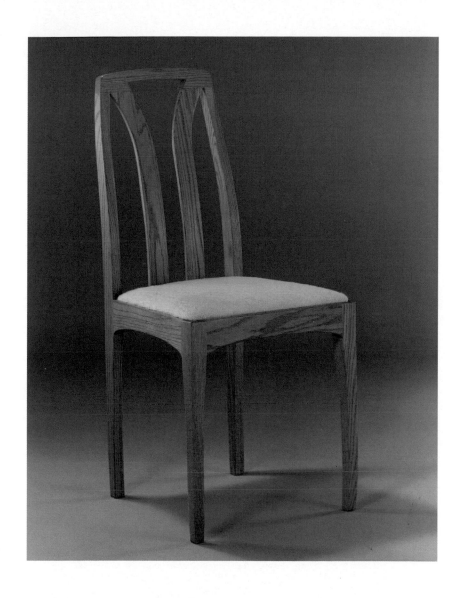

PLATE 5. The chair through which the author began to find his voice,
red oak, 17 × 20 × 37 inches, 1980.

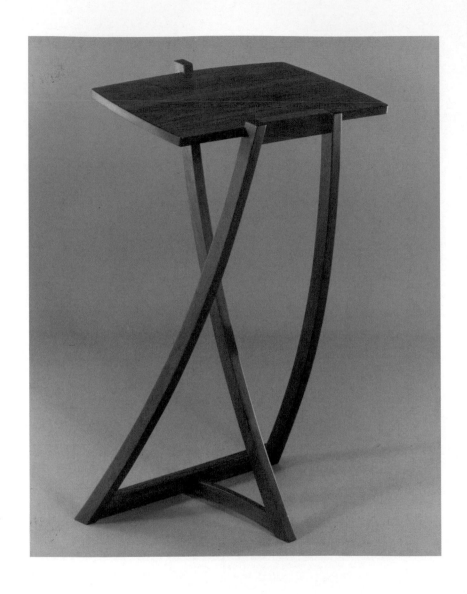

PLATE 6. Dictionary Stand by the author, walnut, 24 × 16½ × 40 inches, 1981.

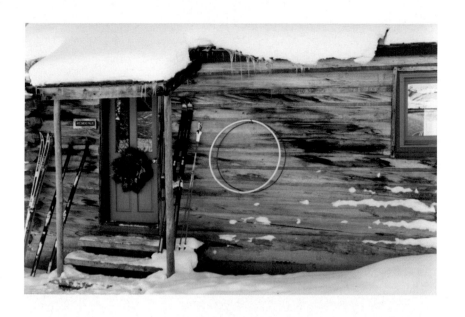

PLATE 7. The author's cabin on the Anderson Ranch campus, circa 1988.

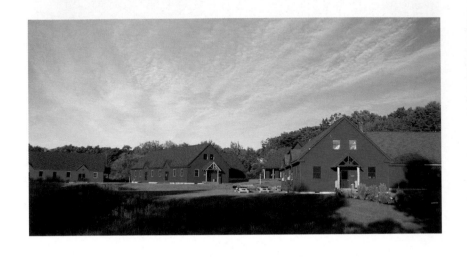

PLATE 8. Campus of Center for Furniture Craftsmanship, Rockport, Maine, 2007.

CHAPTER 9

Second Epiphany

THE FIRST THING I did when I moved to Anderson Ranch in September of 1986 was rechink the old bunkhouse I was given for housing. I pried loose mortar from between the logs, stuffed shreds of
fiberglass insulation into the gaps, nailed on narrow strips of wire
mesh, and troweled on fresh mortar that I mixed from cement, sand,
and water in a galvanized bucket. Snow-capped mountains, awesome in scale, sparkled near and far. Chill air snapped like fresh
laundry in a stiff breeze. Standing on a stepladder at an elevation of
8,600 feet, I felt as if I had been transposed into a new genre. What
would my Eastern European ancestors have made of their seed
blowing so far from the shtetl? Anything seemed possible.

If I was now the Lone Ranger, Chester was my Tonto. A little over
a year earlier I had been doing paperwork at a table in my Manayunk
workshop when I heard footsteps mount the narrow back stairway,
travel the length of the studio behind me, and start down the broad
front stair that I had built during the renovation. I must have been
deep in thought, because only then did I turn around to see who it
was. What I saw was a young, starving, big-boned dog, his long black
coat matted and filthy; he was limping, lonely, lost, and not long for
this life.

I took him in, bathed, and fed him. I called the SPCA and
posted notices in the neighborhood. I paid a vet to give him a good

going-over. Before long the starveling began to fill out into a hand-some prince. Chester looked like a cross between a black Lab and a Newfoundland, with a head broad and solid as an anvil. His arrival had a foreordained quality, as if I'd held my breath for the ten years since Bear Boy's death, just waiting for Chester to walk onstage. For the next thirteen years he would be a companion of Homeric stature.

Chester wasn't the smartest-looking dog – boneheaded would have been a good description – but he wasn't dim. In time he mastered more than twenty different voice commands. He could sit, stay, roll over, heel, come, lie down, drop it, wait, and go. He could distinguish among fetching a stick, a ball, or my slippers. He could jump through a hoop. And although the first time I threw a stick he just looked at it, and the first time we approached a pond he was afraid of the water, a little coaching triggered lifelong passions for both. He would have fetched a stick out of water till he drowned of exhaustion, had I thrown long enough.

Our tiny log cabin (plate 7) was about one hundred feet from the woodshop, across a central quadrangle that was lawn in summer and snow in winter. The quad was also bordered by ceramics studios, a kiln yard, another residential cabin, a photography studio, an admin-istrative office, a gallery, and a print shop. The location made for a public life, especially during the busy workshop season. But from September through May the pace slowed. On a winter afternoon, I could step into cross-country skis outside my front door, hop onto a groomed trail that ran down the golf course behind the wood- shop, and ski miles into the wooded hills beyond a local landmark called Gracie's Cabin. The inrush of crisp air, the sheer physicality of climbing and gliding through a world purified by snow, was rarely less than exhilarating.

Work at the ranch expanded upon the skills I'd honed as a furni-ture maker. I still made one-off furniture, I still tried to design for production, I still maintained machinery and equipment, and I still taught, but I also performed many administrative tasks, all of which were new to me and none of which I expected to like. I prepared budgets, hired faculty and assistants, wrote course descriptions, coproduced the annual course catalog, attended staff meetings, participated on committees to develop policies and plans, drew up student supply lists, selected scholarship applicants, marketed courses, assisted with fundraising, managed a new cafeteria, and more.

Administrative work was quite a surprise. I found that I enjoyed the planning and detail, so long as there was a clear, real-world result to be achieved. Primarily, this outcome was the successful operation of the workshops each summer. But the biggest surprise was how much I took to writing. In high school and college my writing skills had been minimal. Since then I had written only an occasional letter or artist's statement. But at the ranch I wrote course descriptions,

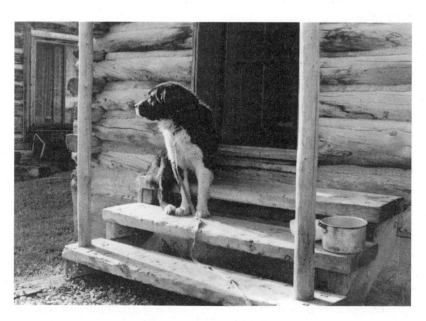

Chester on the steps of the Colorado cabin.

edited the annual course catalog, and became the de facto scribe who took minutes and prepared documents for staff/board committees. In doing so, I began to discover the extent to which words shape events. The language with which I was able to capture a discussion on paper would become the language with which other people understood it retroactively, which in turn determined how they implemented it. At least that was how it felt to me, whether I was writing a description for a twig furniture course or a prospectus for a new artist-in-residence program.

After a year or two, I was persuaded to join a creative writing class by a friend to whom I remain eternally grateful, Laura Dixon. Writing poetry and fiction was another entirely new experience. I was amazed at how readily writing rekindled long-forgotten memories, down to the smell of fallen plums on Nantucket fifteen Septembers earlier. Writing class led to a weekly writers' group. In 1988 I was published – first an article about local woodworkers in *Aspen Magazine*, and then the first of many how-to articles for *Fine Woodworking* and other woodworking magazines. For the better part of 1990, I wrote a weekly column called The Workbench for the *Chicago Tribune*. Ultimately, in 1991, I signed a contract with Taunton Press to write and illustrate a book based on a two-week introductory furniture-making course that I taught annually at the ranch. In contrast to my perennial difficulty selling furniture, it seemed that everything I wrote about woodworking was readily and easily published. It was gratifying to be doing something, finally, that the larger world seemed eager to support.

Daily life at Anderson Ranch was a huge change. Where I had formerly been self-employed, now I reported to an executive director, who reported to a board of directors. Where formerly I had owned my workshop and worked alone, now I worked in a shared facility. Where formerly my personal life had been private, now the comings and goings from my little cabin were community knowledge. I had traded independence for life in a fishbowl.

I didn't get along as well as I would have liked with some of the other fish, either. Partly, it was a cultural problem; I was a brash Easterner among laid-back Westerners. Partly, it was personal; the ceramics director and I spent years puffing and nipping at each other like Siamese fighting fish confined to the same aquarium. Mainly, though, to change the metaphor, I just wasn't well suited to pulling in harness with a team. I kept vying for the lead, even though no one else thought I belonged there. Looking back, I appreciate the effort Brad Miller, our executive director, made to put up with me. One day during my second year he called me into his office to present a written list of incidents where he felt I had been less than respectful in front of the staff. His misery came as a surprise. From my point of view I had been chaffing him affectionately, as I did with my dearest friends.

Still, the upside of living and working in an artists' community far outweighed any downside. Packing ceramicists, photographers, painters, sculptors, printmakers, and woodworkers from a multiplicity of backgrounds into such close proximity was a sustained experiment in creative fission. Prolonged exposure to alternative narratives about life and art, work and meaning caused me to question and revise my own chart of the world. In highlighting our differences, our shared life at the ranch also underlined our commonalities.

Second Epiphany

A few mornings before my fortieth birthday, I opened the worn blue door of my small log cabin and stepped outside into bright winter sunlight. It was 1991, my sixth year at Anderson Ranch. Dry snow crunched beneath my boots as I walked the shoveled path around the perimeter of the quad to the printmaking studio, which was tucked into the concrete foundation of a restored barn. There, among idle lithography presses, the other program directors and I were about to participate in a two-day writing seminar with Arlene Raven, a visiting art critic from New York. Our purpose was to compose personal artist mission statements. Arlene encouraged us to consider our work within the broad context of our lives, and to anchor the language of our statements in the physicality of the materials, tools, and processes with which we worked and the objects that we created.

That night, with the temperature outside freefalling toward zero, I sat at a desk and chair of my own making, knitting words together and raveling them apart. Every few minutes, the silence of the old bunkhouse was broken by the reassuring whirr of a wall-mounted, gas-fired heater. At this point in my life I had been a working craftsman for seventeen years. My original zeal to master the technical skills of furniture making had been succeeded by a passion for the challenges of design. That passion, in turn, was leavened with growing curiosity as to why we make things in the first place. The artist's statement that I wrote for Arlene that night included a sentence that brought my emerging ideas into focus. It read:

> My own values became clear when I eventually realized that the words I used to describe my aesthetic goals as a furniture maker – integrity, simplicity, and grace – also described the person I sought to grow into through the practice of craftsmanship.

This sentence was a second epiphany. For the past decade I had been imagining that my goal was to make furniture that expressed certain values. Now I saw that what I had really wanted all along was to cultivate these same qualities within myself. This was not so much a revelation as a delivery. The central idea – that the primary motive for doing creative work is self-transformation – had been gestating for some time. For me, it would become the key to understanding craft, art, identity, the nature of mind ... the whole tamale.

Toward a Philosophy of Art

Although Anderson Ranch offered workshops in both traditional craft and fine arts media, its board of directors and program staff tended to embrace the prevalent values of the contemporary art world, to the detriment of the sort of craft that I practiced. On balance, they subscribed to an ethos that celebrated novelty and elevated the conceptual while it denigrated utility, beauty, and skill. Within that hierarchy, the instructors I invited for my program (including my personal Mount Rushmore of Tage Frid, Sam Maloof, Art Carpenter, James Krenov, and Alan Peters) were considered stodgy and regressive.

My truth was different. In my gut I knew that woodworkers who design and build one-of-a-kind functional furniture and potters who throw utilitarian teapots and dinnerware are as likely to be exploring, expressing, and prescribing for the human condition as painters and sculptors. The revelation of the Raven seminar provided the intellectual foundation I would need to explore and articulate that position.

The critical point, as I began to see it, was that all people who engage in creative, self-expressive work – visual artists, craftspeople, writers, composers, and others – participate in the same essential human activity as a woodworker does at the drawing board and the bench. None of us enter our studios because the world desperately requires another painting or symphony or chair. But none of us takes the work lightly, either, because it entails too much commitment, discipline, and risk of failure. Those who choose to do it professionally, except for the very few who reach the top, could find more effective ways to earn decent livings. The simple truth is that people who engage in creative practice go into the studio first and foremost because they expect to emerge from the other end of the creative gauntlet as different people.

We may want, as I did, to cultivate personal characteristics such as integrity. We may want to add meaning to our lives by making heirlooms that will keep us alive in family memory down through generations. We may want to feel more sexually desirable, financially successful, or famous. We may want to contribute to saving the world. We may simply want to enjoy a feeling of competence. There are many motivations, often overlapping and not necessarily rational or conscious or even admirable. But whatever our motivations may be, the bottom line is always the same: we engage in the creative process to become more of whom we'd like to be and, just as important, to discover more of whom we might become. We may make things because we enjoy the process, but our underlying intent, inevitably, is self-transformation.

One reason this has proven to be such a powerful understanding for me is that it positions all creative arts as phenomena that originate with the will of the individual. This is quite different from the usual public and intellectual discussion, which tends to focus on the social functions of the products of art – how objects and performances affect their audiences, how they uplift, bind together, sell, signify, inform, ennoble, enrich, enlighten, or interrelate. Surely, it seemed to me in 1991 (and seems to me still), the place to begin to understand the arts is to ask why and how they come into being. The question of what motivates the maker leads one to consider craft and art within the broadest contexts of history, philosophy, biology, sociology, and psychology – perspectives that join art making to the central conversations of our time regarding the nature of humanity.

As I began to see what was common to the creative arts, I could more comfortably acknowledge their differences. All arts may serve their practitioners as vehicles for discovery and self-transformation, but they certainly exercise different human capacities (visual, aural, tactile, literary), employ widely varying types of processes (planned, plastic, intuitive, inductive, additive, subtractive), take place within different fields of ongoing historical conversation, and are accorded differing levels of social status.

Such was the arc of my thought during the years I spent at Anderson Ranch. To a great extent, I credit the philosophy of art that I began developing there with the success of the school I would soon start in Maine, the Center for Furniture Craftsmanship.

CHAPTER 10

Mapping a Craftsman's Mind

THE SUMMER I went to Mexico during college, I drove south to Cuernavaca with my mother and her second husband, Sheldon, who were both Latin American historians. Near the end of our stay, I took a bus to Acapulco on my own – a sleepless overnight journey with an unshaven *viejo* snoring on my shoulder. Just at sunrise I made my way downhill from the bus station. The fabled beach was populated with young Mexicans playing soccer prior to the start of their workday. I lay on my back to watch the scene and was promptly jumped by a group of thugs. They choked and punched me, rifled my pockets and backpack, then strolled away with the meager pickings. Afterward, as nearby soccer players glanced away in embarrassment, I inventoried myself for physical damage, slowly, as one does following an accident, glad not to have been knifed.

It was a strange day. After the mugging I tried to flag down a cruising patrol car on the broad avenue behind the beach, then another, and was simply ignored. Finally, I hailed a stray early-morning taxi to the police station (some of my cash was in the shorts under my jeans) and made a written report to officers, who clearly considered me an annoyance. Then I spent the day walking the length of the Acapulco oceanfront, periodically fording streams of raw sewage that tumbled to the bay from the town above. Every few minutes someone approached to sell me something: paraglide rides, marijuana, sex. One entrepreneur offered me his virgin sister, completely unashamed to be perpetuating a cliché.

That evening I waited at the station for the return bus, barely able to speak for the choking I'd received, sore from being punched, sleepless for thirty-six hours, captive in a foreign culture, and vulnerable in a way I'd never before imagined. A speaker mounted high on the wall played unfamiliar background music until, surprisingly, the score of *Abbey Road* drifted into the room. Instantly, the Beatles tune opened a shutter onto a familiar world. I had the privilege, at that moment, of standing far enough outside my habitual construction of reality to glimpse a portion of it in relief. Viewed from the hard wooden bench of a Mexican bus station, my normal sense of security revealed itself as the dream-walk of an Ivy League college boy. I suddenly understood just how small and illusory a portion of reality it described.

That troubled moment in Mexico would be pivotal to my eventual understanding of why we make things and why creativity matters. It revealed my bedrock sense of reality as fiction, a mythology specific to a particular time and place, in a way I wouldn't forget. Not just rationally revealed – I wasn't observing with the dispassionate awareness with which I am writing (and you are reading) this page. It was a felt revelation, as distant from objective thought as the surge of desire is from a sermon on love.

Before Mexico, I was aware that other people sometimes saw the world askew. I had little trouble discerning *their* blinders. It was only the framework of my own mental cage that remained invisible, much as the walls of an aquarium must be invisible to the tropical fish within – until a mugging smacked my nose hard against the glass. To borrow a term from psychologist Peter Senge, such invisible frameworks might be described as *mental maps*.[23] Their constituent parts – the ideas, beliefs, facts, data, impressions, and suppositions that we carry around in our heads – he calls *mental models*. My own mental map is an unholy scribble. It includes my feelings for my wife, the rules of croquet, the taste of vanilla, the biological characteristics of wood, the tune of a Beatles song – in short, the sum total of what I perceive in the world, how it all connects, and why things are the way they are. These elements fuse into a singular template, which I place over the unfathomable complexity of the universe so that I may point to a few simple coordinates and say, with some conviction, "Here I am, right here!"

Carl Borchert's ideal of a moral life was one feature of his mental map. My father's undervaluation of vocational work was a feature of his mental map. Kendrick's fixation on the female thigh was a feature of his mental map. We all carry such maps around (and they all have their oddities), but like gravity prior to Newton, the phenomenon is so ubiquitous that it often seems to go unnoticed. Or at least we fail to recognize its profound implications. Yet we are born with common, innate characteristics of mind – and my own experience has led me to believe that the most critical, essential, defining aspect of humanity is this very thing. Every person on the planet navigates his life according to a singular, fluid, highly complex mental map that determines his goals, strategies, and tactics, his ideas of selfhood and truth, and his normative and aberrational behaviors – not his drives, necessarily, but how he interprets and chooses to act upon them.

I can be standing in the bench room at school, oblivious to the cacophony of mallets pounding on chisels and the whine of saw blades and planer knives emanating from the machine room next door, until suddenly a quiet *ker-thunk* sends me flying through the swinging doors into the machine room to see if anyone has been hurt. What has taken place in my mind? My mental map, which had been filtering out all of the standard shop noise, has immediately isolated the sound of a piece of wood kicking back on the table saw, brought it to my conscious attention, told me how to interpret it, and guided my response. A non-woodworker's map might not have picked up the sound at all.

This filtering process is an ability that each of us cultivates from birth. We enter the world with minds configured to operate in certain ways but almost completely devoid of data. Survival dictates that we analyze the flood of information that inundates our five senses in order to form useful ideas about what goes on outside the womb and how best to respond. By necessity, we chart our maps with the materials at hand. From the social environment we transcribe stories, ideas, beliefs, and information with which other people have furnished their own mental maps. From personal experience we draw first-hand information with which we revise stories received from others. (For example, my understanding of cancer and my sense of my own mortality changed radically once I experienced Hodgkin's disease.) The acquisition and processing of new information is unremitting; the world does not maintain a steady state. Society and the natural environment evolve continuously, our bodies mature and age, emotions wash through us unbidden. Far from being static, our mental maps can adapt to take all of this into account.

Within my lifetime it was commonplace to picture thought as a completely ethereal phenomenon. Now science tells us that every new idea or piece of information reorganizes neural pathways within our brains. This makes the transmission of information from one person to another a physiological process, comparable to the spread of a virus.[24] Like all living creatures, we cannot shut off sensory intake, and we are acutely receptive to data from our own species. We are so finely tuned to nuances of expression, carriage, speech, and dress that it can take only a glance to accurately place another person within a highly complex sociocultural context. Thus, when you and I interact, your words and actions cannot help but leave a physical imprint on my mind, which in turn may affect my thoughts and actions in ways that are likely to impact still other people's neurons in the future. Ideas and beliefs are hopelessly contagious.

So here's how I think things actually work. The information, ideas, and beliefs with which each person constructs his mental map, from early childhood on, are ladled out of a cultural stew particular to his time and place. He seasons these shared stories with his own experience, or combines old ideas in new ways, to invent fresh understandings that automatically feed back into the social network. In this way, cultural evolution takes place exclusively in the crucible of the individual mind, although it is, in fact, a collective phenomenon. Looked at one way, I operate with a unique mental map and have remarkable latitude of invention within it. Looked at another way, my mental map is so porous to those of other people that I function largely as a cell within an encompassing social organism. Like the scientific model of light, I am simultaneously particle and wave.

From an evolutionary point of view, mental mapping is a biological adaptation, like the saber tooth on the tiger or warm-bloodedness in mammals. The actions of most living creatures are largely determined by instinct, and this narrowly limits their ability to cope with changing environments. Our actions as humans, on the other hand, are determined in great part by the narratives through which we organize the world, narratives that are highly responsive to circumstance. Mental mapping has freed humanity from the chains of instinct in many ways. Almost every action becomes a choice, a decision to be taken or not.

Intransigence

In the early 1980s, as my skills and voice were maturing, the field of studio furniture was swiftly changing around me. One moment I was having exhibitions in fine arts galleries and being publicized in

The New Yorker and *Interior Design*; the next, I looked up from my workbench to find that the spotlight had moved on.

Restrained, functional work that evoked integrity – which could characterize my aesthetic interest – had been news for several decades, starting with Maloof, Carpenter, and their generation of furniture makers. I was riding on their caboose, although I lacked the historical perspective to see it. Ensconced in my Manayunk studio, I was fairly oblivious to the surrounding landscape of contemporary art and design. Still, I couldn't help but notice that more and more of the craft furniture featured in galleries, magazines, and newspapers had a certain flash lacking in my own. Some makers echoed current trends in architecture and product design, such as the postmodernism of Robert Venturi and Ettore Sottsass's Memphis group. Others scaled heights of technical sophistication, eruditely played off heirloom styles, or shorted utility to go long on humor, personal narrative, social commentary, irony, or bravado. The conversation of furniture making was growing lively.

Furniture was doing what ceramics, fiber arts, and other studio craft fields had accomplished in previous decades. It was shattering the remaining constraints of the Arts and Crafts narrative to connect with contemporary ideas and concerns. Yet to me, imprisoned within my own frame of reference, much of that exciting experimentation came across as flamboyant, self-indulgent, pretentious, shallow ... anything but genuine. The most adaptive response would have been to assess the new terrain of studio furniture and ask if there were changes I could implement to move my own design and marketing forward. My actual response was to dismiss the new trends as somehow morally deficient, which allowed me to keep plodding along as usual.

This illustrates an internal tension in mental mapping as it actually works. In theory, my need to accurately understand the world means that I should have readily recalibrated my views to the facts at hand.

In practice, my established ideas and beliefs remain remarkably stubborn. I often invalidate or ignore new information, rather than change my views to honestly assimilate it. One reason for this intransigence, I believe, is that blind faith in one's own certitudes is also an adaptive trait. After all, how judiciously do I want to weigh my assumptions before I decide to exit a burning building? Or, more mundanely, how much time and money should I spend testing every new sharpening method when I have one that works so well already? My need to see the real state of things is counterbalanced by a practical need to make timely choices. The suspicion with which I greeted new design trends in studio furniture was symptomatic of this balancing act.

Design and Decision Making

I often meet people who think that the ability to design is beyond their reach, a mystical gift bestowed on others. Yet over decades of teaching I have seen that design is a skill like any other. As with sharpening a chisel or handling a drawknife, anyone can improve through education, practice, and reflection. To be sure, some individuals are more innately gifted at design than others, just as some are more innately musical or athletic. But there is no reason why the rest of us should not also enjoy the trials and rewards of creative engagement with reasonable success and genuine pleasure, and perhaps an occasional flash of serendipitous brilliance.

Design begins with two things: the intention to create and a problem to be solved. The problem, generally referred to as the *design brief*, may be as specific as the need of a client for a dining table that will seat six people, fit with their existing décor, and cost no more than $6,000. Or it may be as vague as the challenge of making a mirror to reflect one's own taste.

The actual design process consists of methodologies and practical skills for clarifying the brief, generating ideas, and then testing and refining those ideas with an economy of time and effort. My own process, which is fairly standard among furniture makers, starts with pencil (or pen) on paper. Even in the digital era, sketching remains the most effective way to rapidly explore visual ideas in their notional stages. When a sketch sings to me, I have unearthed a promising idea. If it is a sculpturally complex object, such as a chair, I further develop it in three dimensions through cardboard mock-ups, wood scale models, and/or roughly built prototypes. There is no mystery to any of this; one becomes adept at it through practice. The trickiest skill to cultivate in a hesitant student is the ability to hear his own aesthetic response to the visual ideas he is generating.

Design entails a series of aesthetic decisions: lengthen the top, thin the rail, use a figured wood, discard the finial, emphasize a carved texture. To look at a drawing, mockup, or prototype and make judgments well, one must be able to gauge – and trust – one's first pulse of reaction to the arc of a curve, the thrust of a leg, or any other aesthetic stimulus. For me this is a physical perception, as sensate as the touch of a feather. A heartbeat later, that small chirp of internal judgment is joined by a chorus of conscious response (which is useful in its own way, but not the heart of the matter). Design decisions thus combine intuition and deliberation. The choices I make change over time as my mental map evolves. For decades I was enchanted with the color, grain, and feel of cherry. Today I am drawn to rift-sawn white oak. It is not the timber that has altered; it is my aesthetic sense, shaped by the totality of my experience.

A common mistake among inexperienced furniture makers is to move straight from an exciting initial sketch to building a finished piece, without intermediary testing and refining through a considered design process. Certainly that was my mistake for many years, and the result was generally a large investment of time and resources in mediocre work. Even today, when I rationally understand the value of an extended design process, I am strongly tempted to cut to the chase, pull out some boards, and start sawing. Again, two conflicting impulses are at war. On the one hand, good design decisions are reality-based; to make them I need the kind of accurate information that can only be gained through mockups and models that tell me how something will actually look and how it will function ergonomically. On the other hand, being impatient to get to the finish line, I look at my initial sketch and tell myself what I want to hear: it's going to be perfect as it is.

These contradictory motivations are not peculiar to design; they are deeply characteristic of the human mind. Life unfolds as a series of moment-to-moment decisions – small decisions such as ordering breakfast, life-shaping ones such as choosing a career, life and death ones such as electing to undergo a certain treatment for cancer. The more diligence we put into making our mental maps accurate, the greater the likelihood that these decisions will produce the outcomes we seek, and that the outcomes we seek will be truly beneficial. Yet at the same time, we have a compelling desire for psychic comfort, and the reality of things often does not paint a pretty picture. We are ravenous for narratives that portray a world we can feel good about – narratives that address innate psychological needs for context, belonging, order, meaning, hierarchy, and respect, among other things – and we plot our maps accordingly.

Religion is the most obvious type of narrative that addresses such needs – all religions offer authoritative stories of how the world came to be, how it is ordered, how we fit in, and how to lead a meaningful life – but secular institutions and belief systems feed the same appetite, if often in more piecemeal fashion. Whether I am a passionate woodworker, a Red Sox fan, a vegetarian, a Republican, an environmentalist, a Marxist, or a comic book collector, I am ordering my world with an elective narrative that describes how I fit in, nurtures my sense of belonging, and bolsters my identity. The specifics of the narrative I choose are secondary to its psychological functions.

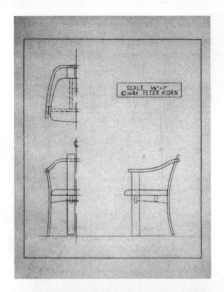
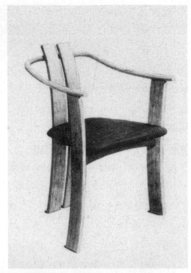
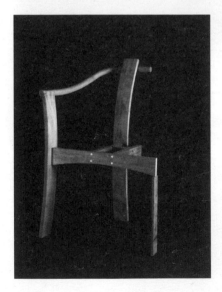
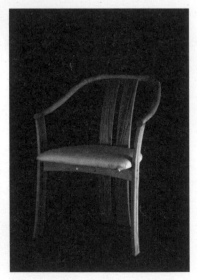

Stages of design development for a continuous-arm chair (clockwise from top left):
plans; rendering of the chair as it would look built directly from the plans;
first mock up; second, sittable mock up.

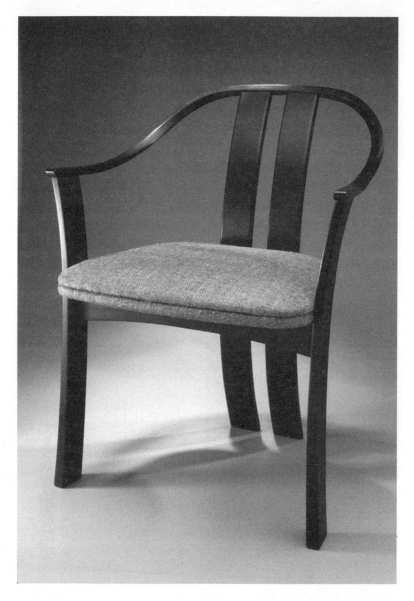

Final, finished prototype of continuous-arm chair, ebonized ash,
$23\frac{1}{2} \times 22\frac{1}{2} \times 33\frac{1}{2}$ inches, 1988.

If I didn't have my current narratives, I would have others in their place. And I would believe them just as fervently.

The structural components from which we construct our world views are so entwined that they are like facets of a single crystal, each presenting a different aspect onto the same interior. *Context* is the larger scheme of things to which we orient ourselves, including our need to understand our origins. *Belonging* is inclusion within a social order, whether it is a relationship with a lover, membership in a family, or allegiance to a nation. *Order* is trust in the predictability of events in the physical and social worlds, and a resulting sense of control. *Meaning* is the feeling that our thoughts and actions make a moral difference in a larger plan. *Hierarchy* is knowing one's place in a pecking order. *Respect* is seeing oneself positively ensconced in the narratives of others.

It would be impossible to overstate the degree to which each of us tailors our mental map to assemble a comforting picture. My saga of becoming a furniture maker was neither more nor less than an extended process of inventing narratives that would provide a sense of belonging, meaning, and so on. Yet at the same time, those narratives had to be anchored in reality if I was to earn a satisfactory livelihood – which they never quite were. I modeled myself on an ideal of the craftsman as a self-employed artisan, working alone, building furniture with integrity to his own technical and aesthetic standards, but I failed to stock my mental inventory with useful stories about how to conduct a business, how to market your work, how to build relationships with customers, how to work efficiently. For twelve years I painstakingly cut every mortise by hand with a mallet and chisels, and wondered why I couldn't earn a decent living!

The unfortunate fact is that mental maps serve more than one master. Healthy survival requires us to see things as they really are. The need to make timely decisions encourages us to stick with what we know. The desire for reassurance encourages us to see things as we wish them to be. When we make a hash of things, as we so often do, it is generally because our yearning for mental comfort has once again trumped our commitment to unbiased observation. Most of the time, the facts of the world knock politely at the gates of our mental fortresses and we pretend not to hear them – a tactic sometimes called cognitive dissonance. On rare occasions, reality busts through our illusions like a Sherman tank. That was the nature of my experience in Mexico. It shocked my mental map into closer alignment with the actuality of things. Creative practice, as we shall see, can be a far more satisfactory way to facilitate the same beneficial result.

CHAPTER II

A Miracle at the
Heart of the Ordinary

NOT LONG AGO I made a new dining table for myself. I was finally done with the rickety antique hutch table that had been rattling plates, sloshing water, and disquieting guests for decades. My design consisted of four turned legs, unadorned aprons, and a thick top made from heavy planks of straight-grained white oak. It's my own take on a traditional form that I hoped would come out sturdy, graceful, unassuming, and, in some undefinable way, generous. A practical table for pleasurable meals.

Turning legs out of three-inch-thick oak turned out to be a challenge. I had designed them with a bead butted tightly under the top block. It's a detail a more experienced turner could have knocked out without hesitation, but I had to make seven legs just to get four good ones. A moment's inattention, an unpracticed hand, and my skew chisel was shredding splinters faster than I could react.

This was creative work, but was it really the stuff of meaning and fulfillment? As I destroyed expensive billets of clear white oak on the lathe through my own incapacity, one after another, I felt frustrated, incompetent, and anxious about what disaster I might unleash next. Yet my will was one hundred percent engaged. My senses were fully attuned to the action of the skew, as unpredictable as a wild animal

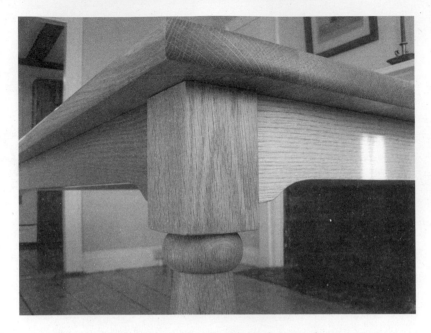

Detail of the bead on a white oak table leg that was a bear to turn.

in my hand; to the rough texture of wood chips as I brushed them off my shirt; to the primal scent of freshly cut oak; to the telltale squeal of end grain spinning against the tailstock, friction-hot. I wasn't radiant with happiness; no choirs of angels were singing. But, absolutely, it was the stuff of meaning and fulfillment.

The Origination of Meaning

Throughout my life I have had dreams in which I could move objects by telekinesis. It felt so natural in the dream that I would sometimes awaken, hold out my hand, palm open, and try to raise a book or candlestick off a nearby table in the same way. Finally, I realized I already had the power to levitate the book and candlestick and float them through the air. I just needed to get out of bed, walk over, and lift the damn things up. In the grand scheme of existence, it's a truly amazing gift. The miraculous in the ordinary!

In trying to understand how creative work functions as a source of meaning and fulfillment, I have also found something miraculous in the ordinary. But first, I had to notice that the ordinary mental effort of sustaining our personal narratives can be difficult and deeply exhausting, however much it may take place out of conscious sight. Not only are we torn between irreconcilable psychic needs, but the actual world bristles with contradictory facts and competing narratives that we work ceaselessly to assimilate, counter, or ignore.

Second, I had to observe that the ordinary path of least resistance is to construct our mental maps with off-the-shelf beliefs for which our societal environment supplies ready confirmation. This could be called the Mr. Potato Head approach, and it appears to me to be the everyday nature of being a sports fan or a political partisan, of watching a favorite television show or religiously reading *The New York Times*, of following the latest clothing fashions or attending church. Immersing the mind in received narratives keeps it comfortably occupied, eyes averted from an indifferent (and ultimately deadly) universe. We are all potato heads to a great extent, but being one doesn't make for a vibrant, fulfilling life.

Third, I had to see that creative practice is a way to proactively challenge and refine one's beliefs on an ongoing basis. I would think this is what Socrates meant by the examined life, and this is precisely what ordinary creative work does. A craftsperson, painter, composer, poet, or choreographer sets out to bring something new and meaningful into the world. He manipulates his medium – be it wood, paint, sound, language, or the human body – in previously untried ways to tease that meaning into being. The result is novel, first person experience that, inevitably, extends the boundaries of his mental map.

Crucially, when I became a furniture maker, I was searching for a good life and a rewarding identity, but I didn't know what a good life would look like or who I would become. Here, I think, is the hidden miracle at the heart of the ordinary in every field of art: creative work is an experiment through which the maker seeks new ways to envision human potential, using himself as the laboratory. This may sound too grandiose to describe daubing a landscape, pecking out free verse for next month's writers' group, or, for that matter, making a dining table. Nonetheless, however minutely we may be absorbed in our own "stuff," through creative practice we are investigating existential questions such as "Who can I become?" and "How should I live?" This subtext gives our actions meaning within the most encompassing of all moral contexts. However humbly, we are participating in the ongoing, communal project of mankind to narrate what it means to be human, how our universe works, and how we should live. Stephen Dedalus expressed this memorably at the close of James Joyce's *Portrait of the Artist as a Young Man*, when he said: "Welcome, O life! I go to encounter for the millionth time the reality of experience and to forge in the smithy of my soul the uncreated conscience of my race."

The Origination of Fulfillment

I may not have been happy turning those seven table legs, but that was no bar to fulfillment. Happiness and fulfillment feel like two distinct states of mind to me, and of the two, I find happiness greatly overrated by those who present it as life's ultimate goal. Whatever it may have meant to philosophers in the past, or to the Founding Fathers who were so intent upon pursuing it, the glow we label happiness today seems relatively inconsequential. We get it if we buy the right car, fall in love with the right person, take the right job, win the lottery, become famous, or eat our favorite candy bar. But then we grow accustomed to our car or lover or job or candy bar … and happiness seeps into the sands of the ordinary. Soon we're hungry for it all over again, and not sure where to find it. Fulfillment, on the other hand, seems to be self-generated through the exercise of our own creative capacities. However recalcitrant the universe may be, when I am creatively engaged I have a sense of purpose and fulfillment that makes happiness seem like a bauble. Ask me if I'm happy when I'm making something in the workshop and I have to stop and think about it. It's not an important variable in the equation.

As a child and teenager I longed for competence, for the ability to do something well in a way that mattered in the grownup world. As a woodworker I found that ordinary competence and something more. I discovered within myself the capacity to transform a wisp of thought into an enduring, beautiful object. I see the same empowering revelation take place in my students today as they perform the miracle of creation. This, I would suggest, is precisely what makes creative practice such a generous source of fulfillment, beyond the pleasure of engaging heart, head, and hand in unison. It exercises one's innate capacity to re-form the given world in ways that matter.

In every religious tradition of which I am aware, the single greatest attribute of the deity (or deities) is creator of the universe. Some people believe that God created man in his own image. Others believe that man invented God as the ultimate projection of human authority and virtue. Either way, the most godlike aspect that both camps recognize in mankind is the ability to create, to forge order out of chaos, to shape oneself and the world in new and, hopefully, better ways. Acknowledging this, one could reasonably say that creative practice produces fulfillment simply because that is how the human species has come to be constituted, whether through evolution or creation. But I would amplify that explanation with the following: everyday creative practice is a process of charting core elements of our mental maps from an independent stance. In doing so, we meaningfully inhabit our selfhood as free-willed agents to the fullest possible extent. Simultaneously, we are actively investigating and informing the shared stories of our society, thus meaningfully inhabiting our selfhood as communal beings to the fullest possible extent, too.

Creative fulfillment is not something to achieve and keep, like a college degree or an Olympic medal. It resides in the process of making the table, not in the satisfaction of sitting at it. Without generation, the wires go dead. Although I am not religious, I suspect that religious fulfillment, similarly, does not endure simply because one adopts a system of belief; it requires practice such as prayer, good works, and ritual observance, all of which provide fresh personal experience that bolsters or challenges the believer's narrative. Those who find the greatest religious fulfillment may well be those whose ongoing struggles with doubt engage them in shaping their own narratives of belief. This would explain what theologian Paul Tillich meant when he said, "Doubt isn't the opposite of faith; it is an element of faith," and what philosopher Miguel de Unamuno meant in saying, "Faith which does not doubt is dead faith."

In ninth-grade anthropology class, Mr. Platt taught us that the capacity to make and use tools was mankind's defining characteristic. Forty-plus years later, I have arrived at a different conclusion. Mankind's defining characteristic is the construction of narratives that explain who we are and how the world works. These mental maps do not only frame our experience of reality; they actually shape reality, because they guide us as we interact with the world. Meaning and fulfillment, as I've experienced them, come through the independent exercise of this capacity, and creative practice is a powerful way to do so. I could never have imagined, half-listening from the third row, just how transformational the use of tools would be.

CHAPTER 12

Creating a School

A COUPLE OF YEARS into my sojourn at Anderson Ranch, I was surprised to hear my mother lament a loss of focus on my part. There I was, congenially spreading my attention among furniture making, freelance design, writing, teaching, and administrative work, thinking I was making progress on all fronts, yet it looked to her like I was dithering. In the context of my mother's life experience, this made sense. My mother was (and remains) an historian who has ordered her adult life around disciplined research and writing. Single-minded passion was what she knew and valued.

My own sense of things was less dire. I felt like a rushing mountain stream that enters a broad valley to spread wide and placid, with only a vague sense of forward movement. Still, I had an underlying intuition that the multiple currents of my life would eventually sort themselves out for another hurtling leap. I simply had no idea what it would look like.

One of the many future possibilities that began to take shape in my mind was starting a nonprofit educational organization that would stand up for utilitarian craft as a deeply meaningful expression of the human spirit. But I was also exploring other ideas, such as starting a craft dude ranch where people could divide their time between trail riding in the Rockies and learning to build furniture and throw pots. Over a period of four years, I gradually developed the first idea into plans for a nonprofit woodworking school. Among other things, this entailed writing a thorough prospectus, lining up corporate and private donors, thinking through programs and curricula, creating pro forma budgets, and settling upon a location. Anderson Ranch was the conceptual starting point for my thinking, since that was what I knew. My proposal came to include summer workshops, a national awards program, and a publication that would address the why of furniture making, rather than the how. The projected operating budget relied heavily on fundraising, since that was the model at the Ranch. Accordingly, I began to talk to potential contributors, with the goal of finding ten people willing to commit $5,000 a year for three years to get a new school off the ground.

In thinking about location, I identified three critical factors. First and foremost, I thought that being in a destination resort such as Aspen would be critical to attracting summer workshop participants. In addition, real estate had to be inexpensive, since I had almost no capital. Moreover, I personally preferred to live in a relatively rural area and be near the ocean, since I loved to sail. Weighing all these factors, the coast of Maine seemed the best choice, although I had little personal connection to it, having last been there as an eleven-year-old camper at Flying Moose Lodge.

In October 1989, I visited Maine on vacation. In 1990 I returned with my fiancée, Sarah, and in 1991 we returned as a married couple, each year exploring different parts of the coast. In October 1992 I was back again, this time traveling solo, looking at the Camden/Rockport area and staying with an old friend. Camden seemed like a good location, with its attractive mix of mountains, ocean, cultural organizations, and tourist infrastructure, but I was in no rush to make a decision. It would be another year before the book I was writing for Taunton Press came out, and I planned to promote the new school on its jacket. Then, on the morning before I was scheduled to fly back to Colorado, I received a telephone call that kicked my plans into fast-forward.

It was my editor at Taunton Press, calling to tell me that *Working With Wood: The Basics of Craftsmanship* would come out in the spring, six months earlier than planned. Suddenly the future was upon me. Either I opened the school right away, or I missed the opportunity to promote it with the book. That same day I telephoned Sarah to ask, "Can you be ready to move to Maine in two weeks?," then gave notice to Brad Miller, leased a house in Camden, rented a post office box, and arranged for a telephone number. After two frenetic weeks of packing, during which I placed an ad for the new school in *Fine Woodworking*, we headed east. Chester happily watched the country roll by from the front seat of a station wagon trailing behind our rental truck.

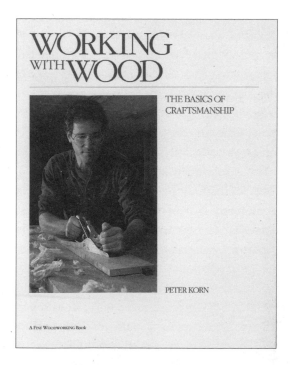

The author's first published book, 1993.

All of the disparate threads of my working, creative life – furniture making, teaching, writing, and administration – would fuse into building a school. The placid stream had resumed its rush to the sea.

Maine

When fate declared that it was time to open a school, my nonprofit plan was still rising in the oven, although I prefer not to call it half-baked. I had found only five of the ten benefactors needed, and was a long way from having all the necessary pieces in place. Instead, working with what little I had, I moved to Maine to offer courses on my own under the oversized marquee "Center for Furniture Craftsmanship" and see what happened.

On a raw, sleety November day, Sarah and I moved into a small rented house on the outskirts of Camden. For the next couple of months, I made it my full-time job to scour the real estate market, trying to find a property within my budget that would work as a small school. Finally, we settled on a respectable old farmhouse with an attached barn in the nearby town of Hope. As soon as we had the house under contract, I printed a trifold brochure that offered seven two-week courses from mid-June through September.

The purchase contract was contingent on obtaining zoning permits. As it turned out, we had disturbed a hornets' nest. At least two of the immediate neighbors were transplants like us, and they didn't want our six-student school in their rural retreat. I conducted a public hearing on site to show that the sound of a table saw ripping through hardwood was inaudible from their houses, but their stated concern about noise turned out to be window dressing. As best we could tell, they were worried about "strangers roaming the neighborhood," which appeared to be code for not wanting black inner-city students walking around. Dramatic zoning hearings ensued, escalating to include lawyers and expert witnesses who testified as

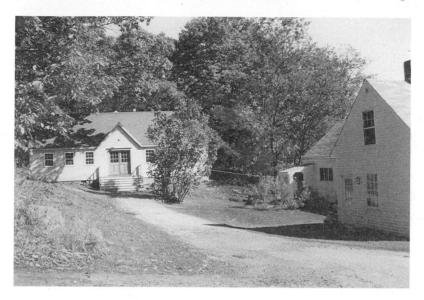

The original school on West Meadow Road, 1993.

to whether our school would adversely impact local real estate values. During the hearings we were vilified and belittled. The town's code enforcement officer referred to me as "Wingnut, over there..." Sarah was in tears.

The zoning board gave us unanimous approval. The neighbors threatened to sue the town. With that cloud hanging over us, I made the hard decision in late March to withdraw from the purchase contract. My rational reason was the uncertainty and expense of the impending lawsuit. My emotional reason was the total evaporation of the hope and excitement with which we had come to Hope. In its place we experienced a sickening sense of foreboding whenever we drove out to visit the property or thought we might run into our future neighbors elsewhere.

It was a difficult winter. Maine is so far east in its time zone that December daylight begins to wane by midafternoon and the sun

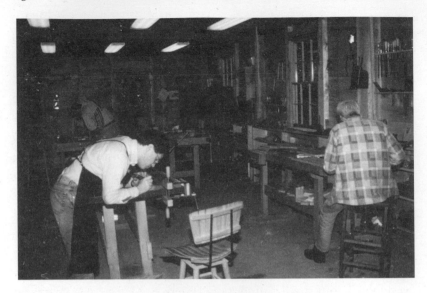

The bench room at West Meadow Road, 1993.

sets at 4 p.m. on the solstice. Some afternoons were so gloomy that I would get into bed, pull the covers up over my head, and just lie there – the first and last time that ever happened! But I only had one shot at opening a school. Not only was I burning through my small savings, I was also putting whatever small stock of professional credibility I had accumulated on the line. If the school that I advertised didn't open, who was going to believe me the second time around?

When I withdrew from the purchase agreement, registrations were coming in for courses scheduled to begin in less than three months. I went back to looking at real estate with redoubled effort. Two weeks later, on April 6, I signed a contract on a two-hundred-year-old farmhouse, set on a south-facing hill overlooking the town of Rockland. We closed on May 5 and the next day broke ground for an addition to the small barn out back. It was a scramble, but on June 28, when the first class of six students arrived, the walls and roof were up (although not yet dry-walled), the wiring and lighting worked, and the machines were in fine fettle. We were off and running.

That summer all seven courses filled, and I used waitlists to add two additional full classes in the fall. We drew more students from California and Texas than anywhere else. About half of the students boarded in our farmhouse – we had three rooms to let – and Sarah provided them with three fabulous meals a day. She ran our boarding house as if the restaurant critic from *The New York Times* was going to drop by at any moment. The whipped cream for the breakfast waffles was garnished with pansies. Lunchtime was my favorite, for the camaraderie. Sarah would ring a bell and we would drop whatever we were working on to sit, talk, and eat – boarders and nonboarding students alike crowded around the picnic table outside or the harvest table in our small dining room. There would be nasturtiums on the homemade potato salad. I never ate so many flowers in my life.

Angels

When classes ended in October, the good news was that we had survived our first year. Courses had filled, students left happy, and we had generated enough income to see us into the winter. On the other hand, superb as she was at running a boarding house, Sarah made it clear that it was definitely not what she had signed on for when we married. Looking ahead, I knew that to survive without income from room and board the school had to grow.

If one reason for our strong enrollment had been the marketing provided by the publication of my first book, another had been lack of competition. At the time, there were only four or five places offering similar workshops in the entire country. My life experience told me, however, that if I was starting a school, plenty of competition was likely to spring up. Whenever I had thought I was doing something original, such as moving to Nantucket after college or becoming a furniture maker, lots of other people seemed to have had the same idea at the same time. That was another reason to keep my foot on the accelerator.

Looking around, I found space for rent in a former blueberry barn on Route 90 in Rockport. It would accommodate twice as many students, but I hesitated to sign the lease. The rent was daunting. At $1,000/month, financial failure would be a real risk. Meanwhile, Sarah was urging me to abandon the school altogether. She wanted me to find a regular job with a steady paycheck – a job I would leave at the office when I came home at night.

As it happened, I had recently joined the board of directors of a local nonprofit gallery, Maine Coast Artists, and was participating on their search committee for a new executive director. As we interviewed candidates, I realized that I was qualified for the job and would enjoy it. Drawn by the allure of a dependable income for interesting work, I threw my hat in the ring. So there I was, with winter coming on, weighing two options. Financial security, a happier wife, and a forty-hour-a-week job? Or financial risk, emotional uncertainty, and life-consuming work?

One of the past summer's students was a businessman from Winnetka, Illinois, named Kully Rohlen. We kept up by telephone and one evening he asked, "If you knew that you would make as much income from your woodworking school as from Maine Coast Artists, which would you choose?" With the question phrased that way, it was no contest. My heart was completely in the school; I just didn't know if I could handle the risk. Kully then made a surprising offer. He would wire $25,000 into a savings account in my name at our local bank, and for the next two years I could draw upon it, as a gift, to whatever extent the school's income fell short of the salary at Maine Coast Artists. With Kully's generous safety net in place, I signed the lease on the blueberry barn and published the 1994 course catalog.

Two years later I would gratefully return his money, untouched and with accrued interest. The school had done well.

The second year's curriculum was much the same as the first's. Five two-week Basic Woodworking workshops alternated with four intermediate-level Craftsmanship & Design courses. But this time around enrollment capacity increased from six to twelve students per course, and I taught every class with a co-instructor. I also tested an idea for a new curriculum by listing a winter "Twelve-week Intensive" in the course catalog. "Who would come to Maine for three months in the winter to study woodworking?" my father asked. "Dad," I replied, "there are 250 million people in this country. I only need eight."

In the event, five people signed up for that first Intensive and we ran the course. My co-teacher was John McAlevey, an accomplished woodworker who had recently moved to Maine from New Hampshire. He became a good friend and for many years would be a mainstay of the school's faculty.

For the third year of workshops, in 1995, I invited highly respected woodworkers to teach most of the intermediate-level courses. Among them were James Krenov from California, Michael Fortune from Canada, and Alan Peters from England. Enrollment continued to be strong, and this time around, eight people took the Intensive.

The dilapidated blueberry barn was located at the busy intersection where Route 17 crosses Route 90. All day long, trucks would downshift loudly for the light and then roar back into gear as it changed. The walls shook with the sound, but no one seemed to mind. The enthusiasm among students and teachers was palpable. It put me in mind of Eastern European universities that held classes "underground" when governments shut them down. Not that we were repressed, but I began to understand the extent to which *people* constitute a school, not handsome buildings and expensive equipment. Still, I kept my eyes open for a permanent base. In the spring of 1995 I found a twelve-acre parcel with a lovely, pastoral feel just a mile up the road. Entering from a curb cut on Mill Street, I saw an expanse of golden meadow sloping gently down to the narrow Oyster River, bordered on all sides by sheltering woods. Over the next year I would sign a purchase contract, design a building with the help of an architect, apply for permits, find creative financing, acquire the property, hire a contractor, put up a 4,200-square-foot workshop facility, and outfit the interior.

Part of the financing came from ten alumni who lent me $5,000 apiece for three years and took free workshops in place of interest. Part came from Kully, who stepped up to the plate once again. It was he who actually bought the land and paid for construction of the building. Then, when it was complete, he sold it to me at cost plus interest. This allowed me to invest proceeds from the recent sale of my former workshop in Philadelphia directly into the Maine property, without paying capital gains tax en route. Had some misfortune come my way that winter, Kully would have been stuck with a large, purpose-designed building, far from home, that had few commercial options besides being a woodworking school. Fortunately, everything worked as planned. The school opened its doors for the 1996 workshop season in a handsome, spacious new home.

Looking around the pristine interior days before the first students arrived, I stood at a pivot point in time. Behind me were the twenty-four years that had elapsed since I began pounding nails on Nantucket – a journey rich in health and sickness, love and sadness, dreams and disappointments, and, always, challenging, engaging work. Before me, sunlight from the meadow outside streamed through large windows to illuminate high ceilings with ample fluorescents, clean white walls, freshly painted floors, orderly rows of brand-new European workbenches, finely tuned machinery, and all of the new cabinets, casework, counters, and shelving that I had just built for hand tools, sharpening stations, sinks, and a library. The building was a lovely ship, poised on the ways. The rooms hummed with promise.

1998

By January 1998, the Center for Furniture Craftsmanship was a solid success. From June through October it offered weeklong and two-week workshops, usually with two classes running simultaneously. In the winter and spring it offered two Twelve-week Intensives, back-to-back. Every year, approximately thirty-five visiting instructors traveled from across the country and around the world to teach more than 250 students from an equally diverse geography. Most workshops ran with waitlists, and I had to turn away scores of applicants for the two Intensives. I carried plenty of debt, but was earning a decent living by woodworkers' standards.

The school kept me busy. I taught full-time as many as forty weeks a year and also took care of all of the registrations, housing arrangements, bookkeeping, marketing, facilities maintenance, purchasing of lumber and supplies, and everything else that took place outside of class. I was at school six or seven days a week and did the office work at home in the evenings and on weekends. None of this was good for my marriage, and Sarah and I were divorced.

The work was all-consuming and had severe costs, but I found the rewards commensurate. I saw students discover their capacities for design and craftsmanship. I developed a rich network of friendships and professional relationships. I witnessed the growth of community and connection among instructors and alumni. Most of all, I had the privilege of being fully engaged in a challenging and successful enterprise in which I strongly believed. The curriculum and culture of the school were oriented to my philosophical pole star, which was to understand the practice of craft as a voyage of self-transformation. This was not an overt agenda, though, nor should it have been. Students came to learn how to sharpen chisels, use a table saw safely, and design beautiful tables, not to meditate on the meaning of existence. Still, creative expression was integral to the curriculum. Even the introductory courses involved students in designing their own projects.

All this was good, but that January I was so tired that on a field trip to Bar Harbor I had to ask another instructor to drive while I napped in the passenger seat. So tired that I scheduled a blood test to see if my counts were normal. So tired that I wasn't surprised when further tests led to a diagnosis of Hodgkin's disease.

Cancer at forty-six was significantly different than cancer at twenty-seven. This time I was an adult, comfortably in charge of my own life, and I had some idea of what to expect. Before deciding on a course of treatment, I contacted two of the country's leading Hodgkin's experts through NIH to ask for advice. It was so unusual for someone to get Hodgkin's disease again after nineteen years in remission that they had no statistics or studies to draw upon. Nor could they say whether this was a recurrence of my initial disease or a whole new contraction of it, like catching a cold twice. What I did learn was that the experimental studies in which I had participated the first time around had led to established protocols, so that I would receive the same chemotherapy at our local hospital in Maine as I would anywhere else. As for my prognosis, the more optimistic of the two doctors gave me a 20 percent chance of five-year survival.

Chemotherapy was still the same debilitating regimen of poisonous chemicals, but there had been advances in their application. This time around I had a port surgically implanted in my chest so that the drugs could be administered without destroying the veins in my arm, as they had the first time. Even better, antiemetic drugs had been invented to keep nausea at bay, and they worked for me. There were days when I drove myself to the hospital for chemotherapy in the morning and taught the same afternoon, though that was pushing things some.

When I found out how slim my chances were, one thing was instantly clear. If I wanted the school to survive, it was time to turn it into a nonprofit. No one in their right mind was going to purchase it as a for-profit business. The hours were too long and the money too short. The best plan I could think of was to ask former students and local community members who had experience in nonprofit governance to form a nonprofit corporation, raise money from alumni to purchase the school, and hire me as director if I survived.

It was lucky that the first person to whom I broached the idea was an alumnus named Al Hume. Al was a vascular surgeon who had recently retired to Maine and was charitably involved with Colby College. Back in Philadelphia he had been a trustee of Episcopal Academy. Had he scoffed, he might have fatally wounded my resolve, but Al's response was immediate and positive. "That's a no-brainer," he said. "All you need are ten people to contribute $20,000 apiece."

The next day a recent graduate of the Twelve-week Intensive, Craig Satterlee, called from Georgia to ask after my health. In the course of our discussion I told him about the conversation with Al and how floored I had been by Al's response, which seemed to indicate a personal willingness to contribute $20,000. All I really knew about Craig was that he was a retired hospital administrator, and I couldn't believe my ears when I heard him say, "Count me in!"

Over the next two months, ten intrepid souls agreed to form a founding board of directors. Few could contribute as stoutly as Al and Craig, but all of them brought valuable experience to the enterprise. They included the school's accountant, my book editor at Taunton Press, instructors, alumni, and a local community leader. In April we incorporated as a nonprofit in the state of Maine and began the arduous process of applying to the IRS for 501(c)(3) status. By summer we had begun to solicit alumni and foundations for contributions. Less than a year later, in January 1999, the new nonprofit legally acquired the school. Meanwhile, following six months of chemotherapy and extensive exploratory surgery, I was declared in remission once again. Gratefully, I donned my new hat as executive director of a nonprofit woodworking school.

Growth

When I originally asked people to form a board of directors, I told them there would be no need for annual fundraising appeals or extensive committee work. The school was already self-sustaining. All they would have to do was review the operating budget every November. Once we made the transition to nonprofit and I was feeling well again, however, I began to have ideas. My goal from the start had been to create a permanent, nonprofit institution to promote craftsmanship as an expression of the human spirit. Now we had taken a huge step in that direction by shifting ultimate responsibility onto the shoulders of a board of directors. But, having done so, I could see that becoming nonprofit wasn't enough. As long as I was the only administrative employee and the only year-round faculty member, the school was hostage to my personal knowledge and network of relationships. We needed year-round faculty and staff to implant the culture of the school in multiple positions so that I became replaceable, and for this we had to grow. With unbelievably long waitlists for the Twelve-week Intensives, we had strong guidance as to what direction that growth should take.

At the 1999 annual board meeting, just ten months after the board took over governance of the school, I presented these thoughts. One discussion led to another, and we entered a rigorous eighteen-month planning process. The final result was an ambitious plan to expand the school's programs, facilities, and staff through a $2.4 million capital campaign. New programs would include a third Twelve-week Intensive, a Nine-month Comprehensive, Studio Fellowships, and a gallery. To house these programs, plus a new office and a library, we designed three buildings that effectively quadrupled the school's square footage. To offset the annual costs of the fellowship program and long-term maintenance of the new buildings, we included a modest endowment goal.

We began soliciting contributions in May 2001. Unfortunately, our timing was poor. The stock market began to slide; then the 9/11 terrorist attacks came along. Two and a half years later, after many sleepless nights on my part, we reached our goal. By the end of 2004 the new buildings were complete, the new programs were operational, and we had hired four year-round staff members. The school was truly transformed. In its new metamorphosis, it would function even better than we had imagined through all the years of planning.

Results

The Center for Furniture Craftsmanship, as I write this, has grown up (plate 8). Throughout the year there are anywhere from twenty-five to forty-eight students on campus, depending on whether there are two, three, or four courses in session. They are taught by a visiting faculty of forty-five outstanding professional makers from around the world. Six Studio Fellows explore new work in the Jackson building. Four exhibitions rotate through the Messler Gallery every year, some of which travel to museums in other parts of the country. The workshops and library are open to students around the clock, seven days a week. Students tally their own lumber and supplies as they need them. The entire edifice is built on trust.

At any given time there are likely to be participants at a wide range of skill levels working in different studios: complete novices, experienced amateurs, professional-track students, emerging

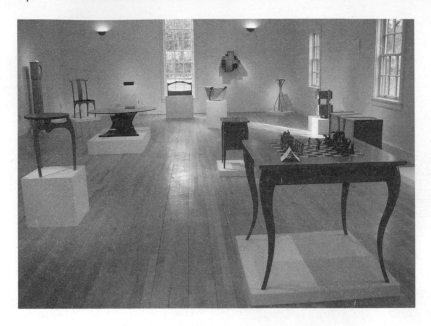

First annual show of student work in the Messler Gallery, 2005.

professionals, and even accomplished professionals who come to
acquire new skills or recharge their creative batteries. Students and
fellows learn from instructors, but they also learn from each other.
Much the same is true for instructors, who escape the isolation of
their personal workshops to share their skills and build relationships with peers from around the globe. The passion on campus is
contagious.

When people ask if I regret giving up ownership of the school,
I tell them it was the best decision I ever made. The Center could not
have become what it is today, had it remained a profit-making ven-
ture. To carry the cost of new construction I would have had to pack
more students into each class, raise tuition enough to price out many
applicants, and/or forego the gallery and the Studio Fellowships –
programs that advance the school's educational mission but need to

be underwritten. As a nonprofit, the campus, buildings, and equipment have been paid for entirely with gifts. We carry no debt and our annual appeal generates a critical 10 percent of our operating revenue. Our growing endowment improves faculty compensation, funds scholarships, supports free bench space for talented young furniture makers in the Studio Fellowship program, and keeps the facilities in good repair without burdening the operating budget. Generous support from alumni, foundations, friends, and corporations allows us to deliver a far better education, at a far more affordable price, than would have been possible in the for-profit sector.

The other major benefit of being a nonprofit, in addition to being eligible for contributions, is that it provides a structure for engaging the expertise and commitment of volunteers in the school's governance and operations. Not only is the board of directors all volunteer, but many individuals participate in other ways, such as staffing the gallery, setting up lighting for exhibitions, serving at events, and tuning up equipment. A school is a community, pure and simple. Nowhere is this more apparent than in the time and commitment that volunteers give to advancing its mission without personal recompense.

Creative Practice within an Institution

Stripped to its bare bones, founding a school has been a process of creating an effective community around an idea that resonates with a societal need. Delivering ownership of the school into other people's hands opened the gates to their emotional and financial investment. The value of craftsmanship as a creative practice was and remains the catalyzing idea, and it is my job as head of the school to keep it front and center, but the form the school takes around that idea evolves in effective new directions with the benefit of other people's judgment and effort. The bottom line is that the school is a successful institution not only because it embodies shared values, but also because it is structured in a way that invites capable people to pick up the harness and pull. They engage their own creativity by having ideas and effectuating them on behalf of the organization.

I have worn many different hats in the process of building the school. These days I spend most of my time at a desk, where I find administrative work to be a far different form of creative expression than making furniture and writing books. There is still the deep magic of dreaming up new ideas, doing the hard work to make them real, and seeing them manifest in the world – I still get to exercise my creative will in ways that are fulfilling and meaningful – but there are huge differences, too. The questions I ask are different, the material I work with has changed, and the process has become collaborative.

The questions I ask as a maker are personal, whereas as an administrator they are other-directed. On the surface, "How can I make a chair that is elegant, comfortable, and durable?" is replaced by "How can we provide the best possible learning environment for our students?" In the subtext, "Who am I and how should I live?" is replaced by "Who are we and how should we live?"

The raw material with which I work as an administrator changes, too. Instead of being wood or words, it is human nature. Person by person, I spend my time building a community of support around the school's mission and the various programs through which it takes shape. That community is made up of faculty, staff, volunteers, students, contributors, and friends. Creating and maintaining a successful institution turns out to be a process of social engineering.

Finally, instead of making all of the creative decisions myself, as I do when making furniture or writing, I make them at the school in concert with others. I may have an idea for an exhibition, a new course, or a visiting artists program, but to succeed these ideas must quickly become collaborative. People invest themselves where they feel a sense of ownership. So I not only try to attach other people to my vision, I also try to adjust my vision to the ideas and needs of other people.

It would be an understatement to say that not everyone likes administrative work. The field of craft is populated with individuals who have not found fulfillment in contemporary corporate culture. Nonetheless, administrative work can be a source of fulfillment when an institution has a mission that is close to your heart and gives you scope for initiative. The satisfactions that working through an institution bring are certainly not identical to those one generates through independent, self-expressive work, but each has its virtues. Working in harness with other people entails considerably more compromise, but the real-world effects of one's inventiveness may be multiplied a thousandfold.

In his book *Birth of the Chaordic Age*, VISA International co-founder Dee Hock writes:

> The truth is that a commercial company, or for that matter, any organization, is nothing but an idea. All institutions are no more than a mental construct to which people are drawn in pursuit of a common purpose; a conceptual embodiment of a very old, very powerful idea called *community* ... Healthy organizations are a mental concept of relationship to which people are drawn by hope, vision, values, and meaning, and liberty to cooperatively pursue them.[25]

It has been my privilege, for the decade-plus during which the Center has been a nonprofit, to participate in an ideal community such as Hock describes. I could not have asked for more than to see the best in human nature brought forth through a shared passion for craftsmanship.

CHAPTER 13

The Creative Cycle

ALTHOUGH MY FATHER was convinced that I would find manual work unsatisfying when I took up carpentry right out of college, my career eventually developed into one for which he had more enthusiasm. My inability to earn a living as a furniture maker pushed me to become a furniture maker who also taught, wrote, and ran a school. In this new incarnation, thinking with things became the lesser part of what I did professionally. Still, I remained deeply engaged in the conversation of craft.

As I have come to see it, there are three different contexts in which one can participate in a creative field. For shorthand, I call them the first-person, second-person, and third-person voices. You participate in the first person when you explore new ideas by making things yourself. You participate in the second person when you interact with the ideas of others through a direct response to the objects they have created. You participate in the third person when you engage with someone's creation at a remove, through language and images, as when listening to someone explain a technique on television, seeing a craft object in a magazine, or reading about a craftsperson in a book. So far we have looked at the first two contexts, making and responding, as personal, visceral ways of thinking with things. Here I will suggest that engaging with craft in the third person is equally central to the conversation.

These three contexts are not unique to the arts, of course. They describe the evolution of ideas in every field of endeavor. First, through experience and experimentation, an individual cdits, amplifies, and amends the socially prescribed narratives with which he conceptualizes his world. Second, as others are exposed to his revised beliefs through the objects, words, or actions that embody them, their own narratives are altered to a greater or lesser extent. Third, if the new narrative elements are of sufficient interest, they spread to a wider audience through language and images and so become embedded in the culture, where they serve as springboards for the creative output of future individuals. Thus, Michelangelo's *David* serves as a thought marker for almost every artist I know, although relatively few have visited the Galleria dell'Accademia to see it in person.

This same process of creativity and cultural dispersion is described by Csikszentmihalyi as follows:

> To achieve the kind of world we consider human, some people had to dare to break the thrall of tradition. Next, they had to find ways of recording those new ideas or procedures that improved on what went on before. Finally, they had to find ways of transmitting the new knowledge to the generations to come. Those who were involved in this process we call creative. What we call culture, or those parts of our selves that we internalized from the social environment, is their creation.[26]

In arenas such as commerce, publishing, and art history, most people, most of the time, engage with craft in the third person. The effort to "break the thrall of tradition" can be a source of meaning and fulfillment for those who engage with craft primarily through language and images – vendors, writers, art historians, and others – much as it is for those with sawdust in their hair and clay under their fingernails.

Craft in the Marketplace

It may sound odd to speak of craft functioning at a third-person remove in the marketplace, since at a gallery or craft show you can touch a wall sculpture, lift a teapot, or sit on a chair. Yet much of commerce takes place through representation, too. When I encounter an object in a magazine or on a Web site, the thing itself is not there. In its place I have a facsimile in the form of words and images that have been tailored to advance someone's agenda. Even when I encounter a craft object in person at a commercial venue, such as a gallery, auction house, or craft show, I relate to it differently than I might at someone's home or in a museum. In the marketplace, the object is understood first and foremost as a commodity to be bought, sold, and owned. The price tag contextualizes it to serve the seller's ends. The voice of the merchant overdubs the voice of the maker.

I am not implying that commerce is shameful. There is rarely a point in time at which a craft object occupies a vacuum of artistic purity, free of someone's wants and needs. It enters the world tethered to its maker's agenda, which may well include commercial intent, before being cut loose to serve the needs of others. Most of the professional makers I know began their careers with minimal financial aspirations beyond bringing in enough income to be able to create the next piece of work. Still, salability was an aspect of their design briefs from the start. Generally, it only became more so as their needs and responsibilities expanded with age.

Nor would I presume that a vendor's motivation is entirely, or even principally, commercial. Many individuals who market craft are impelled by enthusiasm for the work, the desire to advance the careers of the makers they represent, and even the hope of making the world a better place. Certainly this describes the most respected and influential crafts marketers I have known (or known of), among whom are Bebe and Warren Johnson, who founded Pritam & Eames furniture gallery in Easthampton, New York, in 1981; Toni Sikes, who founded The Guild in Madison, Wisconsin, in 1985; and Garth Clark, who founded the Garth Clark Gallery for ceramics in Los Angeles in 1981. On the Pritam & Eames website, the Johnsons provide an account of their early years that touches upon motivations that were scarcely limited to commerce:

> Although the gallery's first years were a financial struggle typical of a shoestring venture, the partners consider their timing extremely fortuitous. It was during this period that resilient friendships were forged with many of the furniture makers. During this first decade, the Johnsons' small house was often filled with visiting furniture makers who lived in a style similar to theirs. Many shared a '60s background fueled by the belief that you can make a living by doing work that you love, and that such work would be valued by others. The challenge for these artist-craftsmen, then as now, is how do they make this work their own? Pritam & Eames has been privileged to be in place to learn more about why these gifted individuals do what they do and to be there for them as a showcase for their ideas in progress.[27]

Commerce is far more than an exchange of goods between those who make and those who acquire. The Clarks, Sikes, and Johnsons of this world bring their own hopes and dreams to the table. Just as makers create to construct meaning and identity for themselves, and buyers purchase to bolster their personal narratives, so vendors shape their own identities through the exercise of taste and the conduct of business. Taste, after all, is a matter of defining oneself through one's likes and dislikes, and the craft merchant exercises taste above all else in selecting his inventory. When he has to choose between giving floor space to work he loves or work he knows will sell, he may be wrestling with the same tension between exploring new ideas or rehashing old ones with which a maker grapples. To the extent that a merchant challenges the status quo – by promoting innovative work, by inventing new business models, by reaching new audiences – he alters social consciousness. In such cases, selling, like making, starts off as a search for identity and ends up as an empowering way to act upon and reconstitute the world.

The marketplace serves as an engine of distribution and exchange. At its best, it effectively supports the exploration of new ideas and brings them before a substantial audience. Advertising, media coverage, and other forms of marketing disseminate a product like pollen on the wind. Although such marketing mostly takes place in the third person, through words and images, it exposes many more people to art objects than would ever experience them in person. In effect, commerce enables the maker to communicate with society at large. The maker says, "Here are objects that express what I've been thinking about. Do they engage you enough to pay for them and fund further investigation?" Society votes yes or no with credit cards, cash, and checks.

If I seem to be equating products with ideas, it is because every manmade object embodies the worldview from which it originates. I have already argued this in regard to craft, but it seems equally true of industrial products. When I buy a simple loaf of bread, I am purchasing a complex thought marker – a bit of nutrition imbued with the narratives of wheat growers (how and why they grew it), commodities traders, grain silo operators, transport workers, bakers, advertising professionals, store owners, etc. Not every pair of hands through which wheat moves to my larder leaves an imprint of equal scope. But the fact that bread has been baked from certain ingredients in certain ways to become sourdough in my kitchen, a boule on the shelf of our local bakery, Wonder Bread at the supermarket, or a bagel at the delicatessen – or even the fact that we eat bread at all – makes it a cultural expression far more than just a quantity of calories, proteins, and minerals delivered to our bodies out of necessity. In a collection of essays titled *Evocative Objects*, Nathan Greenslit says much the same of his household vacuum cleaner: "... we don't consume individual objects; we consume the social order that they belong to. We buy the vacuum; we consume assumptions about gender, households, families, and social status."[28]

Craft objects and manufactured products objectify complexly layered sets of ideas about how the world is constituted and how we think we should live in it. What most differentiates them are the motivations of their makers and the types of questions that impel their creation. The maker of craft (or any maker) is generally a lone individual asking, in part, how life might be lived with meaning and fulfillment. His work is a process of remapping social narratives central to human identity, so the things he makes speak to those issues. The manufacturer, on the other hand, is generally a corporate entity, the management and shareholders of which are asking how to turn a profit, so the things it makes have little existential content.[29]

Either way, whether a product is made by a craftsman or a manufacturer, its commercial success measures the extent to which the narratives it encapsulates resonate with the beliefs and perceived needs of an audience. This might seem to suggest that commercial success is possible only for the creative person who sells out by catering to popular tastes and prejudices instead of exploring new ground. But contrary to being a trap, the tension between genuine exploration and pandering can be a healthy phenomenon. It is true (and sadly so) that the demands of the marketplace quench some makers' sparks. The world shows so little interest in their creative output that they settle for soulless work just to get by, and may come to regard their vocations as dreary jobs. But others manage to maintain their creative passions while earning an acceptable living. Of these you could say that, rather than inhibit their creativity, the pressure to sell has imposed the discipline of relevance on it. The questions they ask, and the answers they find, prove to be of substantial interest to a larger community. Looked at this way, commerce is a self-regulating mechanism of the social organism for propagating, disseminating, and winnowing out new ideas according to their pertinence, utility, and affordability.

Commerce is not a perfect mechanism. Clever promotion can give mediocre work a broad hearing, while more profound efforts may languish due to poor marketing. Human nature being what it is – more receptive to platitudes than provocation – this is to be expected. Nonetheless, commerce is our most effective mass-distribution system for the material expression of ideas.

The Power of Language

The art historian who has had the strongest influence on the field of studio furniture is Edward S. Cooke Jr., the Charles F. Montgomery Professor of American Decorative Arts in the Department of the History of Art at Yale University. What Cooke has accomplished demonstrates the power of engaging with creative work in the third person.

Among other achievements, Cooke co-curated two seminal exhibitions at the Museum of Fine Arts, Boston. The first, in 1989, was titled *New American Furniture: The Second Generation of Studio Furnituremakers.* To create the exhibition, twenty-six contemporary furniture makers were invited to tour the museum's collection of historic American furniture, discuss the meanings and contexts of specific examples, and then make pieces inspired by what they saw. At the time, and wrongly, I imagined there was something disingenuous about the show. It seemed to me that the theme implied a spurious continuity for contemporary studio furniture within the history of American decorative arts. Now I appreciate *New American Furniture* for two important outcomes. One was that it introduced the term *studio furniture* into public discourse, thereby suggesting the existence of a cohesive cultural movement. The other was to legitimize studio furniture among curators and collectors by being the first significant presentation of contemporary craft furniture at a major fine arts museum.

Cooke's second exhibition, fourteen years later, was titled *The Maker's Hand: American Studio Furniture, 1940–1990*. This time around, Cooke and his co-curators sought to chronicle studio furniture as an historical movement. To do so, they imposed a framework of "generations," divided the time span into decades with characteristics such as "freewheeling" for the 1960s, "technofetishism" for the 1970s, and "professionalization" for the 1980s, and detailed a chain of influence among individual makers. To one who lived through much of the period, their account was hugely oversimplified. Nonetheless, it had the positive outcome of giving studio furniture a berth in the official narrative of art history, where the exhibition's vantage point will inevitably be refined and reassessed. This is as close to immortality as a cultural phenomenon is likely to get.

Cooke's intellectual engagement has produced ideas that will permanently affect the ways in which scholars, teachers, students, and the public think of studio furniture. But, beyond that, he has also affected the way in which furniture makers think about themselves. As I tried to show in a previous chapter, studio craft began as a demographic surge, not as an ideology. Makers of my generation had no notion of belonging to a movement. We felt more like voyagers who managed to make landfall on an abandoned continent, only to find a multitude of others exploring the same forgotten shore. Today, thanks in part to Cooke, we retroactively think of ourselves as having belonged to a movement with an implicit ideology and an explicit trajectory. That we self-identify as studio furniture makers is a tribute to the power of ideas, when conveyed through language, to shape awareness on a broad scale.

When an academic such as Cooke thinks with craft, it is both similar to and different from the way that a craftsman thinks with craft. Similar, in an important way, because I suspect that the process of improving established narratives is what makes the work most meaningful and fulfilling. Different, because the academic's grist is a verbal and pictorial account of other people's thoughts and actions, as opposed to direct physical exploration of the material world.

Working in the realm of words comes with risks and rewards. At the workbench I cannot bullshit a plank of white oak or a chisel; as mediums for thought they stubbornly ground me in the actuality of things. At the keyboard, the immateriality of words confers a mixed blessing. On the upside, their imprecision is conducive to wonderful flights of imagination and association. On the downside, that same malleability puts me at risk of ambiguity and self-deception. The strongest suit of thinking with words is its transmissibility, its viral infectiousness. Words disseminate ideas more easily than objects. They have the potential to reach far larger audiences, and reach them in a form that is more readily absorbed. Language can mainline ideas straight into the collective mind, as Cooke has demonstrated.

The Cycle of Craft

Many of us first become aware of a maker, an object, or a craft activity by reading or hearing about it. By the time we meet the maker, experience the object, or participate in the activity, he or it has already been contextualized by someone else. When this is the case, there is almost no way to relate except through a haze of expectations supplied by third parties. The theories of the academic, the marketing of the merchant, the opinions of the critic, the enthusiasms of friends, and our own life histories may all act as filters through which we respond to an object. What, it is worth asking, survives of the maker's original questions and answers?

We have arrived at what I believe is the measure of a truly strong work of craft or art. It must speak with the maker's own voice, clearly and audibly enough to cut through the babble that engulfs it. As Carl

Gustav Jung beautifully put it: "What is essential in a work of art is that it should rise far above the realm of personal life and speak from the spirit and heart of the poet as man to the spirit and heart of mankind."[30]

An object is most likely to speak audibly with its maker's voice when we engage it in person, one-on-one. It is far more difficult to hear the maker's voice through a visual representation of the object. And it is extremely rare for a maker's voice to survive translation through someone else's prose. Yet, limited as images and language are in this regard, they are still the vehicles through which craft informs the widest possible audience.

In a private home, a table by Nakashima or a chair by Maloof might be experienced by tens or hundreds of people a year. In a museum they may be witnessed by thousands or tens of thousands. In a magazine article or in the narration of art history they can be present to hundreds of thousands or even millions. Only in such intangible form can the work of an individual disseminate to a large or influential enough audience to register a significant quiver on the collective consciousness; only then can it inhabit enough people's mental maps to become cultural currency. (How many people, after all, have seen the *Mona Lisa* in person? Yet that particular painting inhabits a niche in the mind of every person I know.) The trade off, of course, is that work experienced in translation cannot speak for itself. The ideas it contains are inevitably watered down or distorted, as in a game of whisper down the lane. This is a simple fact of life, but it has an upside. At the start of this chapter I characterized creative work as a circular dynamic. What I would like to suggest now is that this circulation is a value-added process.

In his book *The Gift*, author Lewis Hyde offers the metaphor of a gift economy as a way to understand artistic practice. His intellectual approach is poetic, by which I mean he uses the ambiguity of the word *gift*, in all its multiple meanings, to weave an appealing tapestry. Creative inspiration becomes a gift because some artists experience it as a form of grace visited upon them from outside. Once received, this gift is nurtured by the inner gift of the artist, the creative genius with which he was endowed at birth. Next the artist shares his work with others – a third gift that creates a cycle of gifts, a gift economy. When the artist lets go of his work, he becomes an empty vessel, open to inspiration all over again. The more he is able to give, the more he is able to receive.

Hyde is describing the same circular phenomenon that Csikszent-mihalyi and I describe, each in our own way. The creative individual is not the fully detached, independent self of modern imagination. One may equally say that he receives his inspiration as a gift, that he is the product and extension of a domain, or that he furnishes his mental map with the models of his time and place. Here is Hyde's description of the connection of the individual to the whole:

> As is the case with any other circulation of gifts, the commerce of art draws each of its participants into a wider self. The creative spirit moves in a body or ego larger than that of any single person. Works of art are drawn from, and their bestowal nourishes, those parts of our being that are not entirely personal, parts that derive from nature, from the group and the race, from history and tradition, and from the spiritual world. In the realized gifts of the gifted we may taste that zoë-life which shall not perish even though each of us, and each generation, shall perish.[31]

Before writing this book, I passionately believed that craft and art originated with the maker, and that whatever vitality they possessed was the result of his creative focus. Now I see the maker as an extension of society, a cell within a larger organism. The issues with which he wrestles are not his alone. They are everyman's. He participates in the conversation of his field and the broader conversations of his culture. The current of ideas passes through him and returns to the body politic with whatever charge he puts on it. To the extent that the maker's ideas are relevant, they pass from person to person (other makers, academics, critics, merchants, collectors, and the general populace), each one potentially adding his own charge, until finally the current returns to the maker, or the next generation of makers, in the form of a new cultural orthodoxy with which to wrestle all over again. Through this dynamic cycle, the conversations of craft and art in all three contexts – first-person hands-on making, second-person visceral response, and third-person abstract consideration through words and images – open doors to new perceptions and new narratives, lead to greater fulfillment for the individual, and have the potential to advance society.

This, too, was expressed beautifully by Jung, when he wrote:

> Art is a kind of innate drive that seizes a human being and makes him its instrument. The artist is not a person endowed with free will who seeks his own ends, but one who allows art to realize its purposes through him. As a human being he may have moods and a will and personal aims, but as an artist he is a "man" in a higher sense – he is "collective man" – one who carries and shapes the unconscious, psychic life of mankind.[32]

CHAPTER 14

A Good Life

During the years I have worked on this manuscript, writing has been the primary creative medium through which I attempt to explore my perceptions, embody them in the objective world, and communicate them to others. Yet, having once fully inhabited the identity of furniture craftsman, and now also working through an institution, I find that working with wood, words, and people are all different forms of the same essential endeavor. All are ways in which I actively participate in thinking my own self and our shared world into being.

From the beginning, furniture making seemed miraculous because it was a process through which spirit became flesh. A chair that began as a mere glimmer of inspiration would finally stand before me and everyone else, concrete, permanent, useful, and perhaps delightful. As a writer, I have come to see that language is much like wood: a medium through which I think. But I have also come to recognize that language and thought are actually two separate things. I think with whatever is at hand, and words turn out to be only one among many possible media.

Every man-made thing, be it a chair, a text, or a school, is thought made substance. It is the expression of someone's (or some group's) ideas and beliefs. The two-hundred-year-old, double-hung, six-light sash window in the wall opposite my desk, out of which I am looking at this moment, embodies ideas about houses and how we should live in them, tools, technologies, standards of craftsmanship, nature, and much else. It is a material manifestation of the collective consciousness of its time and place, as channeled through the individuals who commissioned and made it.

The plain truth, to which we generally pay insufficient attention, is that our ideas and beliefs determine the nature of reality. I don't mean this as a mystical hypothesis – the maple tree that I see through the age-distorted panes of my sash window did not originate in someone's mind, and it would be there whether or not there was anyone to observe it. What I am saying are really two related things.

One is that our beliefs determine how we personally experience the world – determine reality as we perceive it. I experience the thing before me as a maple tree because of where I pin it on my mental map. Within that map, my model of maple tree exists as a dense linkage of information, memory, and emotion. As a child, I would peel apart the maple's wing-like seedpod and stick it to my nose to become Pinocchio. As a boy, I hid in the maple's branches with a slingshot to ambush passing cars with crabapples. As a woodworker, I am intimate with the grain, density, feel, and working properties of its timber – I have inadvertently cut my finger by sliding it along the squared-off edge of a maple plank, so hard and dense is the wood. As a reader, my imagination has been impregnated with trees: with the stout English oak of Nelson's royal navy, the supple yew of Henry V's longbows at Agincourt, the shifting Entwood of Tolkien's *Lord of the Rings*, and the tree of knowledge in the Garden of Eden. The maple outside my window has an independent existence, but I can only see it through the scrim of my particular and personal mental map.

The other thing I am saying is that our beliefs shape the actuality of the world. Man may not have created the maple tree I see through my window, but he certainly has influenced the conditions that determine the specific form it takes. He cleared and sculpted the land where it took root, and he alters (however inadvertently) the climate that regulates its growth. The world outside my window, like the window itself, is very much a product of the human mind.

With such awesome power comes accountability. The biological imperative to continuously edit our own mental maps means that, at every moment, we have choice as to how we experience the world and what it will become for us and others. As Victor Frankl says in *Man's Search for Meaning*, his moving book about surviving internment in Nazi concentration camps:

> Man is *not* fully conditioned and determined but rather determines himself whether he gives in to conditions or stands up to them. In other words, man is ultimately self-determining. Man does not simply exist but always decides what his existence will be, what he will become in the next moment.[33]

Modern notions of selfhood amplify our individual responsibilities and opportunities in this regard. In former times, when prevalent mental frameworks sealed the individual within an envelope of community, mapping the world was more of a shared effort. Today, imagining ourselves to be autonomous, we shoulder the burden of psychic self-construction in relative isolation. It must have been far less taxing to assume one's place in the choir than it is to improvise these solos.

When I decided at age nineteen to search for a good life, rather than contribute to society through social work, medicine, or public law, I was aware that I might be deluding myself. Yes, the generous people I saw giving aid and support to others didn't appear to be leading vibrant, fulfilled lives themselves, so it made sense that someone should search for the promised land and try to share the route. But what a rationale for self-indulgence! Now, looking back, I see that I needn't have worried. I am so inextricably connected to everyone else, so simultaneously particle and wave, that to even try to live a good life is to participate deeply and meaningfully in the shared life of humanity.

It is a given that, individually and collectively, we think our world into being. The question is: How do we choose to go about it? Do we passively assemble our narratives from a cultural smorgasbord? Or do we test the recipes of others in our own kitchens? Do we take responsibility for some small portion of the world as we create it? My experience is that steering a proactive course – making the effort to think for myself – has been the wellspring of a good life.

In this respect, I have found the creative arts particularly rewarding. The effort to transform oneself by bringing something new and meaningful into being is inevitably an investigation of existential questions. Not only the self-referential: "Who am I and who can I become?" But also the general: "What is it to be human? How does the world work? How ought things to be?" It doesn't matter whether one explores these questions implicitly, as I did when making furniture, or explicitly, as I have through writing. It doesn't matter whether one does so as a novice or as an accomplished professional. However a person chooses to go about it, creative practice directly challenges the status quo of his mental map, impinges upon his core models of identity, and impacts the beliefs of others.

The beauty of craft is that it is such a holistic way to exercise this capacity. As a craftsman I explore the possibilities of my being and character through discipline and creativity. I root my understanding of my own nature and the world around me in earthly soil – wood, clay, metal, glass, fiber, or any other material – with the genius of my own two hands. The things I make boldly embody my thought process. They are accessible to others through touch, use, and contemplation. They communicate ideas that address essential questions of who we are and how we should live.

I am not proposing that craft, writing, or any other creative art should be everyone's path to meaning and fulfillment. There are countless other ways to think the world into being. My sister, Maggie Hawkins, does so as a professor in the Department of Curriculum and Instruction at the University of Wisconsin–Madison, from which she is attempting, among other things, to foster a new educational culture in Uganda. We each seek the path that works for us.

Having Your Life Together

I don't imagine for a minute that my particular version of a good life would appeal to everyone, but here's what a typical day looks for my fifty-eight-year-old self. I wake up next to a woman I love in a small bedroom with two skylights close overhead. The plaster walls are painted yellow, the wood floor is blue. The house, a cape built in the early 1800s, has small rooms and low ceilings throughout. It perches on a southeast-facing hillside that looks out over Rockland and Penobscot Bay to the islands of North Haven and Vinalhaven.

I get up around sunrise. My wife is still asleep. I brush my teeth and hair, dress, and go downstairs. There I spend a couple of hours writing before I leave for work. We share a study and this is my time to write uninterrupted, except for the insistent coming and going of the gray cat. Breakfast is a bowl of dry granola and a glass of water at my desk.

I drive five miles to work over back roads where I encounter one or two other vehicles at most. Sometimes I pull over to the shoulder to jot down a stray idea that I don't want to lose. Cresting Mill Street, a rolling wooded landscape stretches for miles to the west. On days when I return this way at sunset, the view is spectacular.

The school is a cluster of red clapboard buildings set in a meadow, with trees all around. It has the serene appearance of a Shaker village. It is particularly beautiful against the deep white of snow. Twelve weeks of the year I teach full-time, offering the two-week Basic Woodworking course for which I wrote the text. I no longer teach intermediate and advanced courses because I make so little furniture now; instructors who are working craftsmen have more to offer. When I'm not teaching, I'm in the office doing paperwork, having meetings, and making telephone calls. I supervise staff, hire faculty, plan exhibitions, manage finances, write and produce course catalogs and newsletters, work with the board of directors, fundraise, and more.

I leave work between 5:30 p.m. and 7 p.m., depending on whether I am going to the gym in winter, swimming or rowing in summer, or headed straight home. Most evenings my wife makes dinner, but sometimes I shop and do the cooking. After dinner we play a game of backgammon, I wash the dishes, and we may watch a movie before I shower, read, and go to bed.

Meals are the celebratory milestones of my day. When I was in college I realized that there were certain things I was going to have to do daily for the rest of my life, such as eat and sleep, so I might as well enjoy them. My delight in food, though, has roots that burrow into deepest childhood. My mother was not emotionally effusive. She expressed her tenderness in great part through the meals she prepared. I returned her love by eating heartily. To this day, an ideal winter Sunday is one on which I bake sourdough bread, prepare a *cioppino*, and have friends over to dinner.

What makes this life good, ultimately, is that I spend my days thinking a tiny bit of the world into being, primarily by building a school into a sustainable institution, empowering other people through teaching, and challenging my own preconceptions through writing and furniture making. It is unremitting, demanding, repetitive work. That goes without saying. The material of the world does not bend easily. Yet it is work that exercises creative muscle, work through which I construct my identity and map the world in a way that fulfills me and finds confirmation from others. Quite frankly, when I am at the school, I am in a place where I matter.

When I first aspired to be a competent woodworker, I tacitly assumed that having your craft together would mean having your life together – that virtuosity equaled virtue. That fantasy was dimmed by my first summer at Anderson Ranch, where I finally met master craftsmen. What completely pulled the plug on it, several summers later, was an encounter with Peter Voulkos, the founding father of contemporary ceramics.

It is past 10 a.m. on a crystal clear Colorado morning, with an impassive blue sky overhead. I am stationed outside a large, spanking-white tent on the quad at Anderson Ranch, waiting to be of assistance if and when the star attraction arrives. For over an hour, as the temperature inside the tent has risen, the mood of the seated symposium audience has deflated. Through the lowered tent flaps I can feel their sense of anticipation sour into confusion and irritation.

Finally, invisible to the audience, a white van careers down the gravel walkway and pulls up on the lawn. I am the only witness as the driver walks around, opens the passenger door, and the legendary Voulkos falls off the seat, straight to the ground, as loose as a sack of potatoes. The driver, who is about my age, seems unfazed. He steps around the sprawling heap and slides the rear passenger door open. From inside he lifts out a small dog that has no hind legs. He puts a tiny cart down on the lawn and gently settles the dog's rump upon it. The little dog enthusiastically wheels itself along, hits an uneven patch of ground, and overturns. There they lay, side by side in the grass. The hapless dog on its back, front legs flailing; Voulkos, prone, muttering, apparently the worse for alcohol or drugs, both of which he was infamous for abusing.

Twenty minutes later, Voulkos is finally positioned at a potter's wheel on a platform in front of the audience. There, addled as he is, he throws a mammoth wedge of clay with a mastery that no other ceramicist in that tent, or perhaps anywhere, could likely summon. The clay is so outsized that the steel legs of the potter's wheel break through the plywood of the platform under its weight, and the demonstration resumes on the ground. Witnessing his suddenly sure hands and body at work, it is apparent the clay has summoned a gift that flows through Voulkos like an electric current.

Peter Voulkos was a master craftsman, but master of his own demons he was not. He was known for liberating contemporary ceramics by punching holes in otherwise superbly crafted pots, and what better metaphor for the man himself than the flawed vessels he created? What, then, does all my vaporing about craft as a profound source of meaning and fulfillment amount to? Let me be clear: people who are creatively engaged are not necessarily happier, more fully realized human beings than the rest of us. To master a craft is not to achieve a state of enlightenment, despite my youthful expectation to the contrary. Creative practice simply makes our lives richer in meaning and fulfillment than they might be otherwise. For some of us, creative practice may be among the few slender threads that bind our lives together at all.

Just as it doesn't guarantee having your life together, neither does being adept at a craft or any other creative art necessarily make one an especially likeable person. How do we relate to someone who subordinates every other aspect of his life to the pursuit of his own creative path, which is generally what a "master" has done? I have been that person for most of my adult life, and there is no question that my commitment to my creative interests often disappoints the reasonable expectations of emotional engagement others may harbor. I have not been the best of husbands, the best of friends, or even the best of dinner companions.

Making the internal commitment to bring an idea to fruition can be a scary proposition. There is a moment, sometimes at first light, when a long-germinating idea crystallizes in your mind and rings true in your bones. For me it might be a design for a chair or a vision for a new program at the school. You think: If I commit to this idea, it will consume my life for the next five weeks, or the next five years. It's like seeing a snowy peak, beautiful in the distance, and deciding to hike there. You know there are likely to be unseen valleys, daunting inclines, and treacherous terrain ahead of you. You know that once you're en route there will be few open vistas such as this one to encourage you. You even know that if you manage to arrive, what you'll see is not the mountain under your feet, but still another peak in the distance.

My father sang a song to me, and then we would sing it together: *The bear went over the mountain* (repeated three times). *And what do you think he saw? He saw another mountain* (repeated three times). *And what do you think he did? The bear went over the mountain …*

And on we'd sing. And so it is. As a maker you put one foot in front of the other and you own the journey. Finding creative passion that governs your life may be a curse as well as a blessing, but I would not trade it for anything else I know.

Endnotes

1. Pirsig, Robert M. *Zen and the Art of Motorcycle Maintenance*. Bantam New Age Books, 1974, page 25.
2. Sennett, Richard. *The Craftsman*. Yale University Press, 2008, page 9.
3. Zuger, Abigail. "The Brain: Malleable, Capable, Vulnerable." *New York Times*, May 29, 2007.
4. Erhard Seminars Training was the first of the new age, cult-like, consciousness-raising organizations to gain traction nationally.
5. Throughout the text, where I employ *he*, *his*, and *him* to make generalizations in the third person singular, those generalizations are intended to be gender neutral.
6. This observation comes from an essay titled "The History of Craft," by Paul Greehalgh, in *The Culture of Craft*, edited by Peter Dormer, Manchester University Press, 1997.
7. *Ibid.*
8. These observations are found in the essay "Workmanship: The Hand and Body as Perceptual Tools," by Polly Ullrich, in *Objects & Meaning: New Perspectives on Art and Craft*, edited by M. Anna Fariello and Paula Owen, Scarecrow Press, Inc., 2005.
9. Ruskin, John. *The Stones of Venice*. Merrill & Baker, 1851, page 164.
10. Pasztory, Esther. *Thinking With Things*. University of Texas Press, 2005.
11. Leach, Bernard. "Belief and Hope." 1951, as credited at www.leachpottery.com.
12. From the article "Amateurism, Art, and Absorption," in *Crafts* magazine, Sept./Oct. 2008, page 53.
13. Csikszentmihalyi, Mihaly. *Creativity*. HarperPerennial, 1996, page 107.

14. *Ibid.*, pages 110–13.
15. Crawford, Matthew B. "Shop Class as Soulcraft." *The New Atlantis*, Number 13, Summer 2006, page 9.
16. Chuck Close, in an interview with National Public Radio's Terry Gross on April 14, 1998.
17. Taylor, Charles. *Sources of the Self.* Harvard University Press, 1989, page 105.
18. As quoted by Charles Taylor (page 84 of *Sources of the Self*) from Murdoch, Iris, *The Sovereignty of Good*, Routledge, 1970, page 80.
19. From *Education of a Woodsmith*, by Art Carpenter, edited by Tripp Carpenter and Linda Moore, Bubinga Press, 2010.
20. Csikszentmihalyi, Mihaly. *Creativity*. HarperPerennial, 1996, pages 48–50.
21. Painter Georgia O'Keefe gave voice to this when she said, "The abstraction is often the most definite form for the intangible thing in myself that I can only clarify in paint." O'Keeffe, Georgia, *Some Memories of Drawings*. Viking Press, New York, 1976.
22. Pasztory, Esther. *Thinking With Things*. University of Texas Press, 2005, page 93.
23. From *The Fifth Discipline Field Book*, by Peter Senge, Art Kleiner, Charlotte Roberts, Rick Ross, and Brian Smith, Doubleday, 1994.
24. Pinker, Steven. *The Blank Slate*. Viking Penguin, 2002, page 65. Pinker writes, "We should understand culture, according to the cognitive anthropologist Dan Sperber, as the *epidemiology* of mental representations: the spread of ideas and practices from person to person. Many scientists now use the mathematical tools of epidemiology (how diseases spread) to model the evolution of culture. They have shown how a tendency of people to adopt the innovations of other people can lead to effects that we understand using metaphors like epidemics, wildfire, snowballs, and tipping points. Individual psychology turns into collective culture."
25. Hock, Dee. *Birth of the Chaordic Age*. Berrett-Koehler Publishers, 1999, pages 119–120.
26. Csikszentmihalyi, Mihaly. *Creativity*. HarperPerennial, 1996, page 317.
27. Found at www.pritameames.com/archives-1.html on May 24, 2009.
28. Turkle, Sherry, ed. *Evocative Objects: Things We Think With*. Essay by Nathan Greenslit, "The Vacuum Cleaner," page 139.
29. Yet, conversely, manufactured products such as smart phones, in their soulless multiplicity, wreak far greater change on the collective psyche than do contemporary art and craft.

30. Jung, Carl Gustav. *Modern Man in Search of a Soul.* Routledge, 2005, page 172.

31. Hyde, Lewis. *The Gift.* Vintage, 1979/2007, pages 197–98.

32. Jung, Carl Gustav. *Modern Man in Search of a Soul.* Routledge, 2005, page 173.

33. Frankl, Victor. *Man's Search for Meaning.* Beacon Press, 2006, page 131.

Selected Reading List

Adamson, Glenn *Thinking Through Craft* (Berg, 2009)

Alfody, Sandra, editor *Neocraft: Modernity and the Crafts* (The Press of the Nova Scotia College of Art and Design, 2007)

Auther, Elise *String, Felt, Thread: The Hierarchy of Art and Craft in American Art* (University of Minnesota Press, 2010)

Becker, Ernest *The Denial of Death* (The Free Press, 1973)

Bellah, Robert N. *Habits of the Heart* (Harper & Row, 1985)

Bruner, Jerome *Acts of Meaning* (Harvard University Press, 1990)

Carpenter, Art *Education of a Woodsmith* (Bubinga Press, 2010)

Crawford, Matthew *Shop Class as Soulcraft: An Inquiry into the Value of Work* (The Penguin Press, 2009)

Csikszentmihalyi, Mihaly *Creativity: Flow and the Psychology of Discovery and Invention* (HarperPerennial, 1996)

Csikszentmihalyi, Mihaly *Flow: The Psychology of Optimal Experience* (Harper Perennial Modern Classics, 2008)

Dissanayake, Ellen *What is Art For?* (University of Washington Press, 1988)

Dormer, Peter, editor *The Culture of Craft* (Manchester University Press, 1997)

Fariello, M. Anna Owen, Paula Owen, editors *Objects & Meaning: New Perspectives on Art and Craft* (Scarecrow Press, Inc., 2005)

Frankl, Victor *Man's Search for Meaning* (Beacon Press, 2006)

Hock, Dee *Birth of the Chaordic Age* (Berrett-Koehler Publishers, 1999)

Hyde, Lewis *The Gift* (Vintage, 1979)

Koplos, Janet and Metcalf, Bruce *Makers: A History of American Studio Craft* (University of North Carolina Press, 2010)

Krenov, James *A Cabinetmaker's Notebook* (Van Nostrand Reinhold, 1976)

Lucie-Smith, Edward *The Story of Craft* (Phaidon Press Limited/Cornell University Press, 1981)

May, Rollo *The Courage to Create* (W. W. Norton & Co., 1975)

Meyer, Marilee Boyd, editor *Inspiring Reform: Boston's Arts and Crafts Movement* (Davis Museum and Cultural Center, 1997)

Pasztory, Esther *Thinking With Things* (University of Texas Press, 2005)

Pinker, Steven *The Blank Slate* (Viking Penguin, 2002)

Pirsig, Robert M. *Zen and the Art of Motorcycle Maintenance* (Bantam New Age Books, 1974)

Pye, David *The Nature and Art of Workmanship* (Cambridge University Press, 1968)

Senge, Peter et al. *The Fifth Discipline Field Book* (Doubleday, 1994)

Sennett, Richard *The Craftsman* (Yale University Press, 2008)

Steinberg, Michael *The Fiction of a Thinkable World: Body, Meaning, and the Culture of Capitalism* (Monthly Review Press, 2005)

Tavris, Carol and Aronson, Elliot *Mistakes Were Made* (Harcourt, Inc., 2007)

Taylor, Charles *Sources of the Self* (Harvard University Press, 1989)

Trow, George W. S. *Within the Context of No Context* (Little, Brown and Company, 1978)

Turkle, Sherry, editor *Evocative Objects: Things We Think With* (The MIT Press, 2011)

Yanagi, Soetsu *The Unknown Craftsman* (Adapted by Bernard Leach) (Kodansha International, 1972)

Index

ABOUT THE AUTHOR

PETER KORN is the founder and Executive Director of the Centre for Furniture Craftmanship, a non-profit woodworking and design school in Rockport, Maine. Born in 1951, Korn grew up in Philadelphia, where he attended Germantown Friends School and majored in history at the University of Pennsylvania.

A furniture maker since 1974, his work has been exhibited in galleries and museums across the United States. In addition to writing *Why We Make Things and Why It Matters: The Education of a Craftsman*, which won the 2014 Maine Literary Award, Korn is the author of several how-to books. These include the bestselling *Woodworking Basics: Mastering the Essentials of Craftsmanship* and *The Woodworker's Guide to Hand Tools*.